PLEASE FEED ME

PLEASE FEED ME

a punk vegan cookbook

BY NIALL MCGUIRK

SOFT SKULL PRESS

Please Feed Me

© 2004 by Niall McGuirk

Cover and book design by Amanda Luker
All photographs by Ricky Adam & George Curran

Published by Soft Skull Press
New York, NY
www.softskull.com

Printed in the United States of America

ISBN 978-1-932360-09-7

Cataloging-in-Publication data for this title available from the Library of Congress

CONTENTS

I wasn't quite sure what to write when Niall asked me for my take on the whole Hope thing. When I thought about it, I realised it was a really powerful influence on my life. I wonder, if I hadn't gone to see Not Our World in 1989 and stalked Niall until he asked me out, what would I be at now? What amazes me about Hope is the amount of people it touched, whether they liked what Hope stood for or hated it. A lot of people had experiences good and bad. >>

FOREWORD

Abhinanda

It changed my viewpoints on a lot of things and probably the direction my life took. My decision to become vegan was based on an awareness that probably originated in music. It is now a very big part of who I am. I've had two healthy pregnancies resulting in two very healthy vegan children. At times I have questioned why I do it but once I sit and think about it for any length of time I realize there is no other way for me to live. I hope my children will feel the same way when they grow up and not give me a hard time for not conforming to how and what others choose to eat.

The funny thing is, at the time, I didn't realize just how good it was. Like most things, it's only when you look back that you remember the good and filter out the bad, but it really was mostly good. My experiences or memories were a bit different to others in that my favorite bit was hanging around outside the gigs and just chatting to people and having a laugh with Valerie or whoever. I enjoyed cooking for the bands and, in latter days, the endless arguments at the Hope meetings. Then there are all the amazing people I've been lucky to meet that have become life friends. I hated putting up posters, as that involved traipsing around town and being a nuisance, but it had to be done.

THE FUNNY THING IS, AT THE TIME, I DIDN'T REALIZE JUST HOW GOOD IT WAS.

I don't think the scene in Dublin is the same now. That's not to say it was better then, but venues for smaller bands are nonexistent and I just don't think people would dream of going to places like The Grattan, The Attic or Barnstormers—they really were dodgy. The venues now are very "trendy and cool."

Niall has talked about this book for so long and I kept thinking "yeah, yeah, in twenty years you'll have the time to do it," but he has proven me wrong. Here I am the night before it's due to go to the printers and I'm writing my piece. I have to say I am so proud of him, as he has written it at a time in our lives when there are more demands on us than ever before due to two wonderful, awe-inspiring, but very energetic children. For some time now we have worked in shifts and Niall has spent many nights in front of this screen putting this mighty piece of work together, but it was something that had to be done. Even if it's only for Niall to put on paper what I would say was probably one of the best periods of his life (excluding illness). But I have a feeling more than just Niall and I will look at this time as influential.

Now that his third little baby is out of the way I think he is actually going to miss pestering people for recipes and poring over layouts and what looks best. I am proud to have been involved in Hope and know that I am a better person for the experiences and the people I have met.

–Miriam McGuirk

This is a book about Hope. Although originally titled "Document," it is more than just an exercise in looking back. From its earliest incarnation in the mid-eighties as one Dublin teenager with a telephone, until its later phase as the Hope Collective almost a decade and a half later, the central idea of Hope was always activity, awareness, creativity, and access for anyone who wanted to make a contribution. This newest project is no exception. >>

INTRODUCTION

The Redneck Manifesto

The idea for this book first germinated in 1996 at a Hope Collective meeting. I had been involved in putting on gigs since 1984. It was felt that it'd be a good idea to document what had gone on in Dublin. We decided to ask any bands that came through Dublin from then on to donate vegan recipes and I would write up a piece about each gig.

Why vegan recipes? Well, **Flux of Pink Indians** wrote about "my soul for the sole of your shoe" on their *Neu Smell* 7" and that inspired me to change my eating habits for life. I gave up eating meat in 1984, at around the time when many others were doing so as Morrissey had encouraged. After six years of eating dairy products but no eggs I decided that it was only logical for me to turn vegan. As not agreeing to cruelty to animals was my reasoning for giving up flesh I could not find words to support the cruelty involved in the dairy industry. I read up on what food groups are important to eat and have not looked back since.

The story of Hope and how I came to put on gigs is condensed over the next few pages. In the first version of this book we had a recipe AND a related story for each gig but we decided to shelve that for the re-print. If you're interested in it then contact me and I can send on more details.

"IF YOU'VE SOMETHING TO COMPLAIN ABOUT YOU'VE SOMETHING TO CHANGE"

In 1983, inspired by my brother's record collection, local punk band **Paranoid Visions**, the music of British political counterparts **Crass** and **The Partisans**, I was one of three idealistic young teenagers from the north side of Dublin who got a band together. Together we would change the world. We saw music as a means of getting across a message through fun.

BEST OF ALL, THOUGH, WAS THE FACT THAT HOPE CREATED A GENUINELY FRIENDLY AND WELCOMING ATMOSPHERE FOR THEIR GIGS.

We bought a **Clash** book so we could do some **Clash** songs. We called ourselves **Vicarious Living** after a line by a song from **Flux of Pink Indians** and were ready in no time to play some gigs. The question was then, how to get a gig?

I had been to a gig in a bar called Tommy Dunne's Tavern. I rang up the manager and asked could I book two shows for my band. To my astonishment he said yes and that was it.

Some other friends had formed a band and we asked them to play. We borrowed equipment and pestered all our friends and associates to go to the gig and to our surprise 70 people came along. During the second event Deko, singer from **Paranoid Visions**, got up on stage and sang along to one of our songs. We felt it couldn't get any better than this. This is what being in a band was all about. It was that easy.

"HOPE"

Armed with the confidence of putting on a gig I then set about questioning why my favorite bands weren't coming over to Ireland. I loved listening to punk music and its D.I.Y. (Do It Yourself) message was starting to take effect. Bands were no longer waiting on major record labels to release their records. They were creating their own labels and releasing their own music. I wanted to be a part of that community and felt I could help bands travel over to Ireland and play. I contacted people who were active in Dublin and offered to help them. It then evolved into people from outside Ireland getting my name as a contact.

Some friends and I were talking one evening and I suggested we pool our resources together and try and create something. We wanted to give it a title and the name Hope arose. It was just a name but to me it could symbolize all sorts of positive possibilities. We put on gigs and always asked people to help. We wanted to be part of a community and wanted all those who went to the gigs to feel part of it.

I came across **The Pleasure Cell** when I heard about a lecture they were giving on the perils of drug abuse to students in Bolton Street College. After the lecture they played a gig. I was enthralled that not only was a Dublin band playing great music but that being in a band meant more than just playing music to them. **The Pleasure Cell** brought out their own 7" and was completely supportive of anyone at their gigs, always ready to talk and always friendly.

"JUST DO IT YOURSELF"

After **Vicarious Living** split up, my friend Hugo asked me to join his band **Kill Devil Hill**. Whilst doing his fanzine he came across John Robb, editor of another 'zine called *The Rox*. John was also lead singer in the **Membranes**. Hugo asked John why they hadn't played Ireland and he said that nobody had asked him and it grew from there. Simple as that.

Hugo rang numbers from the *Hot Press Yearbook* (a book containing contacts for many venues around Ireland) and asked if they were interested in a British band playing. He got a good response from venues in Drogheda and Limerick. He then booked a venue in Dublin, Belvedere Hotel, and asked bands of a mixture of musical genres to play. All readily agreed and the gig was a huge success—with over 200 people there.

The Membranes were delighted to be able to tour another country and see places they'd never been to before. Getting paid was just a bonus. We traveled around Ireland with **The Membranes** and got to experience their contagious enthusiasm.

When **The Membranes** wanted to return to Ireland and Hugo no longer wanted to be involved, I was more than willing to help out. I rang some venues and arranged for them to stay in my friend's parents' house.

I asked the editor of *Sunny Days* fanzine, Morty McCarthy, to book a gig for them in Cork. I booked them three Dublin shows. When John Robb got back to England (he was now a journalist in the British Music Press) he told everyone he knew in bands (which was an awful lot of people) that they should visit Ireland. That lead to a lot of phone calls and interest.

When people say to me that it's easy to say "just do it yourself," I think back to those **Membranes** gigs and my first gig with **Vicarious Living** and remember that that's exactly how we started. The only guarantee given to the band was that they would receive all/any money that was made on the night. Most were happy with that arrangement, as they would get to visit Ireland, let people hear their band, AND possibly get some money for it. Perfect.

Fugazi was the band that got things going for Hope. My friend Alan, who always seemed to know everything about American bands, learned that **Fugazi** was touring Europe. I immediately wanted to see them but didn't want to travel to England for the privilege. I rang Southern, the British distributor for Dischord Records, who gave me a phone number for Jabs, a promoter based in Nottingham. I rang Jabs and enquired about getting **Fugazi** to play and he was immediately interested. When it came to the issue of money Jabs asked how much was the venue to hire and PA and posters. He then said the band wanted a door price of £3 so we did the calculations and said if there were 180 people at the gig the band would get £200. On the night there was a little less but we put some money together and gave the band £200. The second time they played I was amazed afterwards when we went to count the money with their singer, Ian MacKaye. There was a lot of money left after paying for the venue and associated bills. Ian said, "How about we take this amount and you use the rest to do other things?" After receiving his reassurance that it was OK I said fine/thanks a million. As a result of having that money as back-up Hope then got to put on a load of great bands, give them vegan food, a place to stay for the night, and at least cover their ferry fare regardless of crowd numbers. Oh yeah, we got to release a record, too. **Fugazi** assisted in that happening and Dublin owes them a great debt.

For their fourth visit to Ireland we decided that we would make the **Fugazi** gig a bit special. As their last visit was to a sold-out venue we figured we'd have to get a bigger place and were pretty sure that people would go. So we asked would they play a benefit for Act-Up and we booked the Jesuit-owned SFX using Trinity College as a cover. The agents who practically monopolized the SFX weren't too impressed. Pressure was put on the owners and in turn on us to cancel the gig. The ticket for the gig acted as an information leaflet about AIDS awareness (something not seen at many gigs), including how to use hypodermic needles. It cost a lot of money to print and it caused a lot of controversy. The Jesuits wanted the ticket withdrawn. They said that some of the information on it was too explicit for them. We agreed to print a second ticket (which we showed to the Jesuits—but the original tickets stayed in circulation) and the Jesuits, realizing they had no legal reason to do so, reluctantly agreed NOT to pull the plug, giving their final decision one week before the gig.

To have **Fugazi** from America, **Chumbawamba** from England, and **In Motion** from Dublin all playing in the 1300-capacity SFX (one third usual price for a gig in the venue) I felt we really could do anything we wanted to, once we did it together.

HOPE 2

The **Vandals** got the ferry into the country as foot passengers and we got the bus out to Dunlaoire to meet and greet them. We brought them back into the city by public transport. It just never occurred to us to do it any differently. We didn't have our own cars and always travelled by bus, so why should a band who had just experienced a gruelling boat journey be any different? That innocence may have turned bands away a little bit. Maybe.

THE ATTIC

I was diagnosed as having post viral fatigue syndrome (M.E.). It left me seriously lacking in energy. If I did any small exercise I got severe muscle pain. My parents bought me a typewriter and I got to work on doing a new fanzine (*Sketch*). I spent the little bit of energy I had on writing letters.

It has always puzzled me as to why music is so inaccessible to people who aren't old enough to drink in pubs. Most folk start off in bands when they are under 18 but there is nowhere for them legally to play. The only way to get no age restrictions at a gig was to play it in the afternoon. Andrew Bass asked if I was interested in getting bands to play in The Attic. For £30 one could get the room and a sound engineer. It sounded interesting and they agreed to try out Sunday gigs with no age restrictions, starting at 4 pm. I thought the best thing to do was to have a series of benefit gigs leading up to Christmas.

We handed out leaflets at each gig but other than raising money I often wondered about the long term value of such events. This made me think about how we sometimes don't bother with things because on a wider scale they seem so unimportant. Giving £90 to the Rape Crisis Center is a minor amount by their standards but they really appreciated the effort. It's the gesture, the small step, that counts. Whenever I think about my small world not making a difference, I am reminded of that. Even though the cynic in me suggests that benefit gigs change nothing the optimist believes that someone may relate to it, somewhere, sometime.

The Attic wore its title well. Located upstairs in the small White Horse Inn, it could fit 30 people comfortably and 100 people very uncomfortably. **Green Day** played there on a wintery Sunday afternoon. They took off their trousers and 40 people saw it all. Retrospectively when people talk to me about Hope they mention three bands: **Green Day**, **Fugazi** and **Nomeansno**. If all the people who say they saw **Green Day** when they played with **Dog Day** in The Attic were actually there then the already unsteady floor in the venue definitely would have collapsed. On the day we lost £50 and the floor was perfectly safe. It's kind of novel to be able to say that, but I would much prefer if I were able to give you a recipe from the band.

All regulations went out the window the day **Therapy?** played. Len, the manager, was very worried that his pub would be closed down but still they continued to serve beer. **The Whipping Boy** played the following week and had nearly an equally good crowd. **Green Day**, **Babes in Toyland**, **Jawbreaker**, **Whipping Boy** and **Therapy?** are among some of the bands Hope put on that went on to sign major label record deals.

MAJOR LABELS

Hope didn't want to be part of the major record labels' machinery for their bands. We had no guest list at our events, we tried to treat all bands the same, the same way we treated people who paid in to the gigs and anyone involved in helping with a gig. This way there was no "them" and "us." For us to put on a band tied to a major record label would have been a sign of support for the band, something we didn't want to do through our shows, regardless of individual personal feelings.

If Hope could stay outside the major label machine as much as possible we could show people inside and outside bands that there was an alternative. So major label bands were turned down and not approached. It wasn't a snub or a judgement. It was just something we wished to do. It also left us open for contradiction, something people are only too willing to point out.

The Attic's management was tiring of the afternoon gigs with no age restrictions. A new, slightly bigger venue called Charlie's approached me about putting on shows. They said they would go with Saturday afternoon gigs and would agree to let in under-18's.

More and more people had been in contact about coming over so we tried to go with a gig every fortnight in Charlie's—a regular no-age-restrictions event. Perfect!

We agreed on a suitable date for **Splintered** to get the ball rolling and **Quicksand** followed a fortnight later.

The best way to publicize the events was to do a newsletter to inform people. Hence *React* was born. It started out as 500 double-sided photocopied A4 pages that cost £20. It proved a good way of getting the word out as I put it in record shops, book shops, and cafés as well as giving it out at gigs. I wrote *React* solely so I could pass on information about bands that people weren't taking seriously. I had heard a lot of good music from bands that weren't getting exposure anywhere. *React* gave me a chance to write some brief stuff about a band and people could take it or leave it. *React* became monthly and spread to 5,000 printed copies. It fizzled out after it became a chore.

Hope then decided to give "loans" to fanzines to help them print their first issues. They then paid back the money out of fanzine sales if they could. Around this time I had the idea of starting a record label, Hope Records. It could act as a platform for Dublin-based bands and provide them with a forum. Dublin had many good bands so it seemed like a good idea to document it. I went in feet first. However, I would not have got into it any deeper if I had realized the work ahead.

"A statement is a weapon in an empty hand" was a line from **The Pleaure Cell** song "New Age." When the idea of a record came about it seemed like a natural honor to have reference to the **Pleasure Cell** song.

ARKLOW/NEW ROSS/KILL/DUNDALK/MONAGHAN

A record shop in Arklow, Co Wicklow had been taking copies of *React,* and James, the manager of the shop, said he could get a venue to put on gigs there.

Paul from Monaghan got in touch with me about putting bands on there. At a **Fugazi** gig a person introduced himself as Murt Flynn from New Ross. He wanted bands to go there and play. He could get a venue and PA and his band could also play. Immediately we started telling bands about it and New Ross became a favorite for many people. These places have popped up at various times, the problem is getting them to stay active. People tend to move on from smaller towns and the folks who are instrumental in organizing things don't stay around forever. On the plus side, though, when smaller towns get bands traveling through the crowds are generally more appreciative.

BARNSTORMERS

Another new venue popped up: Barnstormers, on Capel Street. Barnstormers was owned and run by Hell's Angels so some noise and people who looked a little bit "different" were fine by them. **Spermbirds** was the first band to play a Hope gig there.

WARZONE

The people in the band **Spiny Norman Quartet** helped out with Warzone Collective in Belfast and in turn were very active in creating a community up there. Warzone sprang out of the Belfast Youth and Community Group, which was started by a gathering of like-minded people with an aspiration to find their own centre. They set about trying to obtain funding and finally got a building. After putting a huge amount of work into it, the building played host to a café, venue, rehearsal room and was a general hive of activity. It has been an inspiration for many.

We had an idea that it would be good to have our own place for gigs and tried to figure out the best way of making it happen. Finance came into the equation so we decided to start a co-op and look at ways of getting funding. We expanded the idea into a café and saw that you could readily obtain grants to run a business. Of course the café would be a vegetarian café, a place where the link between our music and our food could be forged.

Everything was coming together except for the main ingredient: a suitable premises. We spent a lot of time putting together business plans, setting up a cooperative, and putting together the relevant paperwork for grants. Many afternoons were spent over coffee discussing the price of potatoes.

We received sanction for grants for the co-op but because we were getting funding everything had to be aboveboard. Therefore any prospective place had to meet all the necessary health regulations (or have the ability to meet them). We looked at many places, got very close to getting one or two. Our closest call came when we thought we had finally found our ideal premises. It was an old restuarant on the quays in Dublin, and had a basement that could be used for gigs. The fire exits met the standard and any necessary changes were purely cosmetic. When our bid was accepted we were over the moon. We couldn't believe it. After two years looking and many hours spent searching for funding we were to finally get our place. We anxiously tried to get solicitors to move on it to get contracts sorted out. We had the deposit and wished to put it down. The auctioneer was stalling, however. Two weeks after our initial bid was accepted we were informed that a higher offer had been accepted.

The sense of disappointment that came over us was completely overwhelming. We were devastated. I had never heard the word *gazumped* before then but now felt the brunt of it. Like defeated soldiers we weren't ready to lick our wounds and fight again. The business world had beaten us. We hadn't the heart to continue. At that stage Hope was basically me, with Valerie, Ross and Miriam helping out when needed (quite a bit). We decided to stop for a while, let someone else do it.

HOPE COLLECTIVE

Derek, from *Gearhead Nation* newsletter, asked if we would be interested in sharing our experiences with some other people. Pete O' Neill from Belfast contacted me saying that **Bikini Kill**, **Bis** and **Team Dresch** wanted to come over and had asked for Hope to do the gig in Dublin.

After a hiatus of about 12 months, Mir and I decided to go along to a meeting in Derek's house. From this meeting the Hope Collective was born. We would make collective decisions about what bands to put on and would try and provide a fun and accommodating atmosphere at our gigs.

We decided to pay optional weekly subs, £2 a week. We could then use the money to put on gigs or have a floating fund in reserve. We were all keen on putting on **Bis** and the others. Before that gig we thought it would be nice to organize a couple of benefits in The Attic as our way of saying "Hope is back". We would do a newsletter for the gig and give out some vegan food as a welcoming present for people.

One week after **Bis** appeared on "Top Of The Pops" they played Charlie's. It was the one and only time a Hope gig was mentioned on the billboards around Dublin. It was listed as an "event of the month" on a generic beer company-sponsored poster. We weren't happy with this and were fuming for a couple of reasons:

1) Hope was actively against using a company to advertise our gigs on pieces of wood splattered around our city, especially a company that has a monopoly on splattering.

2) Beer companies had no interest in supporting the Dublin music scene, only in achieving some recognition from it. This gig started at 3 pm to ensure that there would be no age restrictions at the door and had nothing to do with a beer company, other than being hosted by a pub (an unfortunate but necessary circumstance).

Before the gig we spent 45 minutes removing Heineken banners draped throughout the venue. The owners thought we were insane. They couldn't understand our logic. It was truly awful.

CITY ARTS CENTRE

From our weekly Hope meetings and a chance run-in with Alison, who worked in the City Arts Centre, talk of a festival surfaced. Alison said the City Arts Centre would be interested in co-promoting such a thing and asked for our suggestions.

We spoke about it at length and felt it would be good to have workshops on how to do your own fanzine, how to bring out your own record and even on how to put on a gig. We thought it would be interesting to have a discussion on independent music in Dublin.

It was pretty successful. People absorbed a ton of information as various organizations were invited to set up stalls. Sean gave out information on a record pressing plant in the Czech Republic that wasn't expensive to use. A lot of Irish bands have since given that company business. The gigs had no age restrictions and many people went to the workshops.

Our weekly meetings were still proving a bit of a strain for Miriam and me. We lived 25 miles away and some nights we just wanted to go home after work. When these meetings meant organizing a gig for a band that couldn't care about being in Dublin and were willing to openly complain about our efforts it was disheartening.

It all got to be a bit much when the meetings consisted of arguments over what bands should play what gigs. We tried to have consensus decisions on everything within the group. With that in mind there were some long debates about various mind-numbing topics. It was important to be comfortable with everything the collective did but things ended up taking more time than necessary.

One such discussion was what organizations would we try and raise money for, which was much like the square peg into a round hole analogy. There just wasn't enough time for all the organisations we would have liked to help and many were put on the "must get around to" list. Unfortunately some of these were never dealt with.

When Miriam was expecting our first child, that was a lot more exciting than the thought of a touring band playing. Hope never existed just to be a factory for touring bands and it was starting to feel like that. My feeling that bands no longer cared about where they were playing grew stronger. To many of them Ireland was just another country, Dublin just another city, and to me they became "just another band". The feeling of empowerment from getting a band over to a little island country was no longer there. Miriam was nearly due (our daughter Ellen was born five days after this gig) when **Happy Anger**, from Lyons, played.

The excitement that was to follow for us after Ellen was born has made for a new chapter in our lives. We decided that we would concentrate on that excitement and ensure that this book would tell the story of what happened. A second child (Robert) has since been born and this book became a labour of love. The thoughts of following their progress through life excites (and scares) me. I didn't plan to STOP my involvement in gigs; it just petered out that way.

The feeling, though, of "we can do anything we want, as long as we want it and work towards it," is still there deep down in my gut and this book is direct proof of that. Enjoy reading it and try out some of the recipes; they are very good. Please let me know what you think of it.

niall@thumped.com
Hope: 31 Hazel Road, Donnycarney, Dublin 9, Ireland

PLEASE FEED ME

This was the first gig I was ever involved in. For Christmas 1983 my friend Andy and I decided to get guitars and form a band. A friend of ours, Paul, played drums in Artane Boy's band so we got him involved. We had been listening to my brothers' record collection for a few years and got a **Clash** book so we could do some **Clash** songs. >>

CHAPTER ONE

before hope—the early years

Hal Al Shedad

VICARIOUS LIVING + "SUPPORT" | TOMMY DUNNE'S TAVERN, JUNE 1984

We went to see Dublin punk band **Paranoid Visions** play a few gigs and thought they were brilliant. They weren't professionals, they just got up on stage and made a racket, but they also had stuff to say in their songs. This was great to us. British bands like **Crass**, **Flux Of Pink Indians** and **Partisans** were favorites of ours so we started the band knowing that if they could do it, we could too.

After learning how to play (!) we decided to do a gig. I had been to see **The Gorehounds** play in Tommy Dunne's Tavern so I knew it was available for live music. I rang up the manager and asked could I book two gigs. To my astonishment he said yes, so we were ready. My brother John was drafted in on vocals.

Some other friends had formed a "serious" band (in that they knew how to play their instruments) but they had no name. We asked them to play and put them down on the (handwritten) poster as **"Support"**.

We didn't think about it at the time but that band then called themselves **"Support"** and it made me reflect upon how we use that word all the time in music. It has become a pet peeve of mine, as I felt embarrassed that we had the audacity to label them that way. I know it's just a word but its use can be widely interpreted.

We pestered all our friends and associates to go to the gig and to our surprise 70 people came along. During the second week, Deko, singer from **Paranoid Visions**, got up on stage and sang along to one of our songs. We felt it couldn't get any better than this. This is what being in a band is all about.

VEGAN PANCAKES

Ingredients

- 1 1/4 cups self-rising flour
- 3 tbsp soy flour
- 1 tsp baking powder
- 2 tsp vegetable oil
- 1 tsp salt
- 2 cups water (or more/less as required)

Preparation

1. Combine dry ingredients together in a bowl.
2. Make a well in the centre, add in the oil.
3. Pour the water in gradually, stirring constantly. It should finish up like a thick cream. Add more water or flour if neccessary.
4. Set mixture aside to set—30 minutes or so.
5. Heat a small bit of oil in a pan and pour enough pancake mixture in to cover the pan. Fry evenly on both sides.

"These are deadly, and real easy. You can add vanilla essence, cinnamon or lemon juice to the mix. Eat them with pineapple, lemon, jam or anything that comes to mind.

Alternatively you could add parsley to the mixture, fry up some veg seperately and have stuffed pancakes."
—Niall, Vicarious Living

TROCAIRE BENEFIT | C.I.E. HALL, AUG. 1985

BANANA KEBABS WITH PEANUT SAUCE

The combination of the cooked banana with the peanut sauce is scrummy!

Ingredients

bananas
onion
red bell pepper
mushrooms
olive oil
3 tbsp peanut butter
I cup creamed coconut (grated)
1/4 tsp chili powder
2 cloves of garlic (crushed)
1/4 cup water

Preparation

On skewers, thread chunks of onion, red bell pepper and banana along with whole medium-size mushrooms. Brush with olive oil and cook on a barbecue.

Sauce

Mix peanut butter, crushed garlic, grated creamed coconut and chili powder with the water.

—Colm Fitzpatrick, I Am The Waltons

Vicarious Living lasted for just over a year. We put together a lyric sheet (hand written) and a tape of one our rehearsals and gave it to people. Why? Because **Paranoid Visions** had done something similar, albeit a bit better looking. We played quite a few times with the **Visions** and it gave me a glimpse of how people could get gigs. Folk in towns all over Ireland were asking **Paranoid Visions** to travel and they did. Function rooms would be booked in pubs and the locals would all come out for a night of loud music.

Paranoid Visions were instrumental in bringing bands like **Subhumans** and **Poison Girls** over from England to play and it made me aware of how possible it was to do something similar. It inspired me to find ways of gettting people to do regular things in places where there was no established music scene.

Occasionally there was trouble at the gigs. Sometimes, if incidents had already happened, I was asked by the **Visions** to book venues in my name. I soon saw how easy it was. The mystique behind gig promoting was gone. The only problem was letting people know about the gig.

One venue I had to book was called the CIE Hall, a space for employees of what is now Dublin Bus. It was a large hall with a stage and room for over 300 people. It played host to punk bands like **Disorder** and **Shrapnel** and many **Paranoid Visions** gigs. Invariably though, trouble seemed to occur. It was common to see fire extinguishers being let off there and, inevitably, the hall was soon lost as a venue.

One of the last gigs to be held there was a benefit for Trocaire. My friend Hugo and Morgan organised it with me as a reaction to Live Aid. We asked 13 bands to play and somehow managed to pull it all off, raising £616 in the process and running out of time for **AHouse** to play.

MEMBRANES + KILL DEVIL HILL + PARANOID VISIONS + THE EXPERIMENT + SHARK BAIT | BELVEDERE HOTEL, APRIL 7, 1986

Hugo asked me to join a band with him, **Kill Devil Hill**. He also did a fanzine. While putting it together, Hugo came across John Robb, editor of another 'zine called *The Rox*. John was also lead singer in **The Membranes**. Hugo asked John why they hadn't played Ireland and he said that nobody had asked him and it grew from there. Simple as that.

My assistance to Hugo for that tour entailed mixing flour and water and using it as a paste to stick posters up around buildings in Dublin city. There were no official poster sites at that stage and while it was technically illegal to put up posters there were never any repercussions if you weren't caught in the act. Unlike currently, where one can be fined if caught postering illegally.

Ringing contact numbers for venues listed in the *Hot Press Yearbook*, Hugo asked if they were interested in a British band playing. He got a good response from people in Drogheda and

Limerick; they were willing to give **The Membranes** money to play and also to allow **Kill Devil Hill** to do the gigs.

Hugo then booked a Dublin venue, the Belvedere Hotel, and asked a mixture of bands that crossed musical genres to play. All readily agreed and, with over 200 people there, the gig was a huge success.

The Membranes were delighted to be able to tour another country and to see places they'd never been to before. The fact that they got paid was a bonus. We traveled around Ireland with the band and got to experience their infectious enthusiasm.

TEMPEH ROLLS

Ingredients + Preparation

1. Buy the tempeh from health food shops.
2. Take it home and cut into thin slices. Like bacon thin.
3. Put into a frying pan of olive oil and fry until crispy.
4. Put onto toast (whole wheat bread tastes the best) or brown bread rolls.
5. Eat!

There are some variations to this theme.
1. When frying add a touch of Shoyu (the proper soy sauce available from health food shops).
2. Fry it with little pieces of garlic. . .

"Tempeh is fermented soy beans. It comes in a slab. It sounds disgusting. But its got a brilliant taste if you follow the new soul warriors cooking technique. High in protein and high in carbohydrates, this is rocking road food..."

—*John Robb, Membranes + Gold Blade*

JJ SMYTHS | AUNGIER STREET, JUNE 9 + 16, 1987

TASTY GOURMET PUNK ROCK BAKED BEANS

When the simple things are just not enough, try adding some zest to your baked beans. Just add some chopped onions, even a little garlic, some tofu, some mushrooms, even a chopped tomato or a few slices of red or green bell peppers, and you have a simple punk rock dish transformed into a meal that will impress anyone.

Anything with two ingredients is a winner in my eyes. Preparation time: less than it takes you to read this recipe. This is full of calcium and a great way to get a big slab of tofu into your system, without you even tasting it!

1, 2 X YOU CALCIUM SHAKE

Ingredients + Preparation

1 lb strawberries
6 oz silken tofu

1. Juice the strawberries, if you have a juicer. I use the juice as well as the pulp as that is still tasty and moist.
2. Place juice and tofu in blender or food processor, and blend until smooth.
3. Drink and say yummy.

—*Michael Murphy, The Pleasure Cell*

Kill Devil Hill asked any bands we met if we could play gigs with them. That way we got to sample local Dublin venues like the Underground. This was a small room in a pub, available to hire for £30. It had a PA and came with a sound engineer for your money.

I came across **The Pleasure Cell** when I heard about a lecture they were giving to Bolton Street College on the perils of drug abuse. After the lecture they played a gig. This happened every day for a week and I was there each lunchtime, enthralled that not only was a Dublin band playing great music but that, to them, being in a band meant more than just playing music.

Seeing **The Pleasure Cell** was inspirational. They brought out their own 7" and were completely supportive of anyone at their gigs, always ready to talk and always friendly. **Kill Devil Hill** got to play quite a few gigs with them.

We eventually split up however, as personalities were clashing and I was growing less interested in the music. Jarlath and I started **P.U.L.P.** (People Under Legislative Politics) as a two-piece (bass and vocals with acoustic guitar).

We changed our name to Hope after we heard a record by an English band called **Pulp**. Michael Murphy, from **The Pleasure Cell**

suggested it; he thought it was a nice word. After a few rehearsals we got a drummer and a second vocalist and searched around for a gig. We hired JJ Smyths (after seeing **Paranoid Visions** play there), hung up posters of then-Taoiseach of Ireland Garret Fitzgerald, his photo upside down and with tape across his mouth, and felt ready to take on the world. We didn't last long, however, as people in the band grew tired of it.

The word "hope" hung around, though.

MEMBRANES + PLEASURE CELL + NOT OUR WORLD
NEW BOOKS, MAY 20, 1988

John Robb of **The Membranes** was the musical catalyst for me to start putting on regular gigs. His boundless energy and passion for good music rubbed off.

The Membranes were keen to return to Ireland and Hugo no longer wanted to be involved. I was more than willing to help out. I rang some venues and arranged for the band to stay in Paddy's parents' house.

I asked the editor of *Sunny Days* fanzine how would someone get a gig in Cork. He asked why and then said he could book a venue. As well as the Cork date, we booked three Dublin gigs—one gig for NCAD, as Paddy was in college there, one with **The Pleasure Cell** at the back of New Books in Temple Bar (headquarters to the Communist Party of Ireland), and one in the Underground. When John got back to England he told everyone he knew in bands (which was an awful lot of people) that they should visit Ireland.

That lead to a lot of phone calls and interest from people wanting to come over. When people say to me that it's easy to say "just

do it yourself," I think back to those **Membranes** gigs and remember that's exactly how we started.

The only guarantee given to the band was that they would receive any money that was made that night. **The Membranes** were happy with that arrangement as they would get to visit Ireland, let people hear their band and even perhaps get some money for it. Perfect!

I had started playing in a new band, called **Not Our World** (N.O.W.). We got seven songs ready before **The Membranes** came over. With those seven songs we got ourselves on the bill of all the gigs and did the "tour" with them.

MINT CHICKPEAS

Ingredients

1 can chickpeas
medium onion
1 clove garlic
4–5 mushrooms
salt and pepper to taste
dried or fresh mint
olive oil for frying

Preparation

1. Heat oil in frying pan.
2. Chop onion and garlic and add to hot oil.
3. Add in mushrooms.
4. Season with salt + pepper to taste.
5. Add chickpeas and mint and fry for 5–10 minutes

Serve with warmed pita pockets.

—Derrick Dalton, Mexican Pets

VANDALS + NOT OUR WORLD + 3 RING PSYCHOSIS
THE GRATTAN + SIDES, AUG. 8, 1988

MACARONI & NOT CHEESE

Ingredients

- 3 1/2 cups elbow macaroni
- 1/2 cup margarine
- 1/2 cup flour
- 3 1/2 cups boiling water
- 1 1/2 tsp salt
- 2 tbsp soy sauce
- 1 clove garlic, crushed
- pinch turmeric
- 1/4 cup oil
- 1 cup nutritional yeast flakes

Preparation

1. Cook macaroni per packet instructions.
2. In saucepan, melt margarine over low heat.
3. Beat in flour with a wire whisk and continue to beat over medium heat until mixture is smooth and bubbly.
4. Whip in boiling water, salt, soy sauce, garlic and turmeric, beating well to dissolve the mixture. (The sauce should cook until it thickens and bubbles.)
5. Whip in oil and nutritional yeast flakes.
6. Mix part of the sauce with the noodles and put in a casserole dish.
7. Pour the rest of the sauce on top.
8. Bake at 350 °F for 15 minutes, then broil for a few minutes.

—Derek Grant (Vandals + Alkaline Trio)

My friend Alan always seemed to know everything about American bands. He got to hear that **Fugazi** were touring Europe. He told me they featured people from **Minor Threat** and **Rites Of Spring**, from the Dischord record label. I immediately wanted to see them but didn't want to travel to England for the privilege. I rang Southern, the British distributor for Dischord Records, and asked about **Fugazi**. They gave me a phone number for Jabs, who I rang inquiring about getting **Fugazi** to play. Jabs lived in England and helped get the band gigs there. He said he'd ask **Fugazi** about coming over.

In the meantime Jabs mentioned that **The Vandals** wanted to come to Ireland.

We knew of **The Vandals** from the film *Suburbia*. Although it wasn't a regular film on any of our screens, Alan, of course, had a copy of it. We booked the Grattan at a cost of £40. A person running a club night at Sides asked if **The Vandals** could play there too, so the band got to do two gigs in one night to cover their travel expenses.

They got the ferry into the country that day as foot passengers and we took the bus out to Dun Laoire to meet and greet them. We brought them back into the city by public transport. It just never occurred to us to do it any differently. We didn't have our own cars and always traveled by bus—why should a band who had just experienced a gruelling boat journey be any different? It was that innocence that gave **Hope** its spark but probably also turned bands away a little bit.

The first gig of the night was completely packed and the second one saw more than half the crowd make the trek across the city to Sides. The owners of the club weren't prepared for the audience that the gig attracted and they promptly pulled the plug during the gig. **The Vandals** only got to play one or two songs. No one got a refund. We just went home. That innocence again.

FUGAZI + 3 RING PSYCHOSIS + MORAL CRUSADE + NOT OUR WORLD
MCGONAGLES, NOV. 29, 1988

Fugazi agreed that it would be a good idea to travel to Ireland and play a gig. I booked McGonagles. Some recent Sunday afternoons had been spent there, seeing various British bands that the Warzone people from Belfast had brought over to play. Warzone got George Curran and some friends of his to book McGonagles when bands were traveling over. They booked the venue and helped out on the day. Bands that travelled over to play these gigs included **Carcass**, **Joyce McKinney Experience**, **Bolt Thrower**, **The Instigators** and the wonderfully named (and aptly for many) **Dreadful**.

Alan, Fergus, Paddy, Richie and I went about getting bands to play with **Fugazi** and putting posters up in record shops. We plotted the whole thing out and tried to get a varied line-up of bands for the evening. We even did up a press

Ian MacKaye, Fugazi

release promising "a night of musical mayhem."

When it came to the issue of money Jabs asked how much the venue was to hire. **Fugazi** wanted a door price of £3 so we did the figures and said if there were 180 people at the gig the band would get £200. On the night there were a few less but we put some money together and gave the band £200. They were happy and little did I know it but this was the start of something regular.

POTATO PAKORAS

Ingredients

- 4 large potatoes
- 1 onion
- 1 tbsp veg oil
- 2 tbsp ground coriander
- 1 tbsp cumin seeds
- 1 tbsp turmeric
- 1 tsp salt
- 1 tsp pepper
- 3/4 cup gram flour (chickpea flour)
- water (approx. 1/2 cup)

Preparation

1. Peel the potatoes, chop roughly and boil until soft.
2. Dice the onion finely, fry in oil, add 1 tbsp of the coriander, cook for another minute or two, set aside.
3. Put a pan on the heat and wait until it gets very hot, throw on cumin seeds and toss till they are browned (about a minute or two).
4. Take gram flour, 1 tbsp coriander, turmeric, salt and pepper, and combine in a large mixing bowl. Whisk in about a quarter of a pint cold water, enough to make a thick batter.
5. Mash the potatoes when cooked and set aside to cool.
6. Stir the onion mixture into the potatoes and form small patties (you may need a little flour to help them stay together). Dip into the batter and deep fry till golden, then pop them onto a baking tray and bake in an oven at 400°F for 20 min. (as the gram flour needs time to cook through).

—Michael Mullen, Killercrust, 3 Ring Psychosis + Wheel

KELTIC KONVICTION + NOT OUR WORLD + MALICIOUS DAMAGE + THE LAWNMOWERS | THE EARL GRATTAN, FEB. 17, 1989

MAGNIFICENT SEVEN PASTA SALAD

Ingredients

1/2 lb penne
I medium-sized onion
14 oz can kidney beans
IO oz can corn
I red bell pepper
2 medium-sized tomatoes
some mixed herbs

Preparation

1. Boil pasta until it is cooked.
2. Dice'n'slice onion.
3. Slice tomatoes.
4. Seed'n'cut red bell pepper into slivers.
5. Drain can of corn.
6. Drain'n'rinse can of kidney beans.
7. When the pasta is cooked, rinse'n'immerse in cold water until it has fully cooled.
8. Chuck pasta in a large bowl and then chuck in everything else.
9. Sprinkle with mixed herbs (to taste) and mix well.
10. Now you're ready to eat.

"I often use this salad for taking to work for lunch. Prepare the night before and stick in the fridge overnight in a tupperware container (flavors mix well overnight) and next morning take to work."
—Smeggy Angus

At this stage **Not Our World** were playing regularly in The Earl Grattan, on Capel Street. We were almost turning into the resident band there. We kept being asked to play. There was a group of 20-30 people who always came to see us play and maybe some bands asked us on to their bill so they could be guaranteed those 20-30 £1.50s or £2s.

We decided that we wouldn't play in The Grattan for more than £2 and one evening threatened to pull out of a gig with **The Foremen** as they were charging £2.50. We only found out about it on the night and thankfully they brought the price down. If they hadn't we certainly wouldn't have played but people may have come to see us without knowing.

We were thinking about our admission price policy. A lot of bands were charging what they felt they could get away with, looking for as much as was acceptable. **Fugazi**'s insistence on a door price maximum of £3 helped shape our thinking. It made us be attentive as to why we charged money for gigs. For **Not Our World** it was a matter of gigs being affordable to all and consequently that was the case for Hope gigs too.

We decided to book two Saturdays in the Grattan and have four bands each night.

The first featured **Angus**, Dublin's original Ranting Poet. His poems about Daisy the Cow, *The Sun* newspaper and Ronald Reagan used to have the crowd in stitches but there was meaning in there too. **Angus** was always around and, if ever a band didn't turn up, he was a good man to turn to for an impromptu performance. He was at the gig that night so we asked him to say a few words and added him to the bill.

NOT OUR WORLD + THE BANISHED + HOUSE OF BYRON + ANGUS
THE EARL GRATTAN, FEB. 24, 1989

The two **Not Our World** gigs in The Grattan were full of incident. During the first one there was crowd trouble in the venue but, more worrisomely, there was trouble outside the second week.

Timo played bass in **Keltic Konviction**. He later moved on to **Shred**, where he played with the Bearded Lady and Shane (both from **Not Our World** and who are now in **Joan of Arse**.) The gig he mentions was chaotic. Some people came along just to cause a bit of havoc. This was familiar to gigs at the time. Abusive heckling was a craze but the situation got out of control that night when a glass was thrown on stage.

Timo caught the brunt of it and finished his set with a bloodied head. Thankfully no more glasses were thrown at Hope gigs and Timo had no interest in, or intention of pursing the matter legally (which has happened at other gigs where people have been injured).

The second gig was, again, memorable for the wrong reasons. One of our friends, Susanne, had her handbag stolen outside. She ran upstairs to the venue, visibly shaken. Deko and I went chasing instinctively. We didn't find the culprit and Susanne was very upset. As organizer of the gig I felt responsible, but she got off better than Timo had the previous week.

Those gigs were turning points. Both attracted 150 people, but the trouble made everyone want to make things better. We wanted to be able to go to gigs in peace and not have to worry about safety. Through **Not Our World** (and then Hope) a policy was made to encourage friendliness at gigs, let people see that they weren't just there to be consumers, that they were at a gig to be part of something—something they could find comfort in and something they could be comfortable with. That became the plan, the "hope."

BANACADO

Ingredients + Preparation

This is my baby Holly's favorite meal. I can't think of any recipes for adults. To make it, you get half a banana and half an avocado and mush it all up with a fork. Then you gotta put it in a bowl and feed it to a baby.

"I ain't really sure of any anecdotes from the glory days of Hope. Was the gig I got my head bottled by skinheads at a Hope gig? I remember Niall getting up on stage after it happened and telling the skinheads that if they wanted to glass anyone, to glass him, so I guess it probably was a Hope gig.

I was 17, and really scared. I was never going to go to another punk gig as long as I lived, and Niall convinced me that scary people are not quite as scary if you decide to not be scared of them. I hope that makes sense.

It probably sounds like quite a negative thing to bring up, but it was probably the most important thing I learnt at those gigs. I also learnt that rock'n'roll concerts can be a place where people who feel confused and isolated almost every place they go can feel at home.

You can meet the best friends you'll ever have at cool punk gigs. Almost every friend I have is someone I either met at or through a Hope gig. I certainly wouldn't have ended up promoting concerts if it wasn't for Hope gigs."

—Paul Timoney, Keltic Konviction + Shred + Ultramack

ANHREFN + NOT OUR WORLD | OLD MAN OF ARRAN, MAY 19, 1989

Anhrefn was the first band to travel to Ireland on John Robb's recommendation. They rang me saying they wanted to visit Ireland and play as many gigs as possible. They were a great band to get gigs for. They lived in Caernarfon, near the ferry port in Holyhead, and had their own PA Their costs were low, they could come over for the weekend and play anytime, and people liked them. It made it

BANANA BREAD

Ingredients

- 2 tbsp soy flour
- 1/2 cup water
- 1/4 cup veg margarine
- 1/3 cup sugar
- 2–3 bananas, mashed
- 1/4 cup chopped walnuts (optional but delicious
- 1 3/4 cup flour
- 1/2 tbsp soy flour
- 1 tsp baking powder
- 1/4 tsp baking soda

Preparation

1. Mix the soy flour in with some of the water until creamy.
2. Mix the marg, sugar, bananas, and walnuts together.
3. Add in the soy flour mix and the rest of the water to the marg mixture.
4. Sift in the flour, salt, baking powder and soda. (This means putting the flour through a sieve.)
5. Put mixture into a large greased bread pan.
6. Cook in the oven at 350 °F for 30–45 minutes.

—*Niall, Not Our World*

ideal for getting gigs outside Dublin.

I contacted Morty McCarthy, who had put **The Membranes** on in Cork, and asked if he could find a venue for **Anhrefn**, which he did. I also rang up venues in Donegal saying that I was representing this Welsh-speaking band and managed to find two places that were willing to take them. One was a glitzy hotel in Gweedore where they played as part of the weekend's entertainment. Brendan, Michael, Martin and myself travelled up from Dublin to Donegal. We tried to sneak into the hotel room that **Anhrefn** were given but were caught by the manager. **Anhrefn** gave us the keys to their van where we slept soundly. Unfortunately for them the battery ran out on the van (must have been all that body heat). They eventually got back to Dublin for this gig.

The Old Man Of Arran was an unusual place for a gig but we couldn't find a place for the specified night in our regular venues. We found a pub down by the Four Courts that needed a PA **Anhrefn** duly obliged.

This night was also memorable for me for another reason. On our way home, walking down the Quays in Dublin, we were confronted at knifepoint. We all managed to run to safety and then decided that we'd put no more gigs on in the Old Man of Arran, even though they didn't want us anyway because of the noise.

FUGAZI + SLOWEST CLOCK + NOT OUR WORLD
MCGONAGLES, NOV. 23, 1989

Fugazi was the band that really got things going for Hope. This gig, their second visit to Ireland, was packed out. We were totally taken by surprise. For a while it was looking hairy—**Snuff** were due to play but had to pull out of the gig due to a death in their family so **Slowest Clock**, from Dublin, stepped in at very short notice.

In a repeat of what happened the first time they came over, **Fugazi** missed the ferry. I was playing in the first band and when we went on stage **Fugazi** still hadn't shown up. There were no mobile phones then so my Dad drove into the gig to tell us that Fugazi were in Holyhead at 4 pm and were due to get the next ferry.

In the event, things worked out fine. **Fugazi** arrived in plenty of time, during our set, and literally shook McGonagles that night. The PA kept threatening to fall over and we had to station people to just hold the speaker stands up.

There was a lot of dancing and many people felt they could get up on stage and jump into the crowd at will—something **Fugazi** and plenty of others in the audience didn't want.

I was amazed afterwards when we went to count the money with Ian McKaye, singer with **Fugazi**. There was £1400 left after the venue and PA had been paid. Ian said, "How about we take £550 and you use the rest to do other things?" After receiving his re-assurance that it was OK I said fine/thanks a million.

We used that money to start a Hope fund, money that could be used as a back-up in case things didn't go according to plan. Hope then got to put on a load of great bands, give them at least their ferry fare regardless of crowd numbers, and release a record. **Fugazi** assisted in that happening and Dublin owes them a great debt.

CHOCOLATE CAKE

Ingredients

2 1/4 cups unbleached flour
1 1/2 cups sugar
1/2 cup cocoa
1 1/2 tsp baking soda
3/4 tsp salt
1 1/2 cups warm water
1/2 cup vegetable oil
1 1/2 tsp vanilla extract
1 1/2 tsp white vinegar

Preparation

1. Preheat oven to 350 °F.
2. "Butter" 2 8-inch cake pans with margarine and dust with flour.
3. Combine the flour, sugar, cocoa, baking soda and salt in a bowl.
4. Pour in the water, oil, vanilla and vinegar and stir until well combined.
5. Pour into the 2 cake pans evenly then bake for 30–40 minutes till a knife inserted in the centre comes out clean.
6. Cool on a wire rack for 10 minutes, then remove from pans and let cool completely.

Icing Ingredients + Preparation

1 cup of margarine
3 cups of confectioners' (powdered) sugar
2–3 tbsp of orange juice

Beat margarine till fluffy—add the sugar incrementally and blend. Add the orange juice and whatever sugar remains and continue to blend till spreadable. Ice cake only when it's completely cooled.

—*Guy Picciotto, Fugazi*

D.I. + THE fFLAPS | NEW INN FIASCO, MARCH 1990

The next band Jabs wanted to send to Ireland was **D.I.** The New Inn was a new venue being run by Smiley Bolger. Smiley lived around the corner from my parents and he was infamous, due to his friendship with Phil Lynott from **Thin Lizzy**.

This venue was bigger than the Grattan and had space for people to dance so we decided to book it. It was on the outskirts of the city but we hoped that people would be willing to travel that little bit extra. However, two days before the gig we heard that **D.I** weren't willing to travel at all. They needed to cancel their Irish leg of the tour due to lack of finances, leaving us with a dilemma.

If we were to cancel the whole thing at this stage we would be letting the venue down plus people might not hear about it. They would still go out of their way for no gig. I rang **Anhrefn** to see if they could come over at short notice. They were busy but some friends of theirs, **The fFlaps**, were available. We told **The fFlaps** that we would pay their ferry costs if they could make it for the gig. They agreed so we went ahead with it. But worse was to come.

That night someone managed to sneak into the venue, break a toilet and flood the place. The electricity went so the gig couldn't happen after all. Maybe it was a gig destined not to take place but the results of one person's stupidity had a profound effect. They managed to spoil **The fFlaps** trip to Ireland, ruin many peoples' evening, cost us nearly £300 AND get away with it. The craze of abusive heckling was giving way to toilet smashing.

THAI POTATOES

Ingredients

1 onion
1 potato
1 carrot
1 clove garlic
1 can coconut milk
corn and snow peas (optional)
stock
lemongrass and cilantro
any other optional veggies . . .

Preparation

1. Lightly boil the potato and carrot
2. Fry onion and garlic
3. Add the al dente potato, carrot to the mix
4. Add the coconut milk and corn (and if you are a masochist, the snow peas)
5. Cook some more, and when almost done, add the lemongrass & cilantro.
6. Eat.

"Chef Fin!!! Not."

—*Fin, SMH + Mexican Pets*

NOMEANSNO + KILLERCRUST + NOT OUR WORLD + TRENCHTOWN + SLOTH | NEW INN, APRIL 1990

Nik Evans was the person organizing the British end of a tour for **Nomeansno**. He rang to ask if we would be willing to get the band a gig in Dublin. I was a fan of the band so readily agreed and knew that the New Inn would be perfect. It had plenty of space to allow people to dance.

Unfortunately for me I was also pretty sick around this time. I had been out of work since the previous December and had been diagnosed as having post viral fatigue syndrome. I had little energy to deal with all the intricacies of gig promoting. Other bands had to be contacted, posters/fliers made and distributed. Fergus and Paddy helped out immensely with this one. We decided to meet up regularly in my house and discuss forthcoming gigs. During our discussion it was felt that it would be a good idea to have the **Nomeansno** gig as a benefit.

CHUNKY MONKEY MILKSHAKE

Ingredients

- 1 cup soy milk
- 1 banana
- 1 tablespoon sweetened chocolate powder (Make sure it is labeled parve, which means that it does not have dairy or meat products.)
- 2 tbsp roasted cashews

Preparation

1. Pour milk into blender.
2. Add rest of ingredients. Blend.
3. Drink. Enjoy.

Serves 1.

"Preparation time: 5 min. It's simple but nice and picks you up after you've been beaten down by life. Add vodka to taste."
    —Matt, The Waltons + The Redneck Manifesto

Ian MacKaye, Fugazi

We thought that seeing as there would be a decent crowd there, we could raise some money for an organization, but more importantly try and raise some awareness. Amnesty International seemed a good choice. **Nomeansno** were happy if they got their travel expenses and all other bands played for free. I spent most of **Nomeansno**'s set in a car outside the venue and therfore didn't get to see someone hurting their ankle dancing. They were happy with the £20 we gave them for their taxi fare and their hospital fee.

ohn Robb passed my name on to fellow Mancunians **Babydigger**. They sent me

a tape I thought was excellent. I couldn't wait to get them over to play a gig.

Around this time, people in Belfast contacted me. **Jailcell Recipes** were

coming to Ireland to play and wanted to visit Dublin. >>

CHAPTER TWO

hope—the start

BABYDIGGER + LAWNMOWERS + JAILCELL RECIPES + DRIVE + F.U.A.L. NEW INN, JUNE 7 + 29, 1990

I booked the New Inn for the two gigs. Hope was put on the posters in the hope that people might go along even if they didn't know the bands, as we were the people who had put on **Fugazi**.

Unfortunately this wasn't the case for either gig. There was a miserable turn-out at both. We would have lost a fortune had we been made to pay the full price for the venue. Smiley realized that we were trying and let us off with any short-age we had. We had money left from the **Fugazi** gig that went to pay off the bands' travel expens-es but those New Inn gigs were jinxed. First **D.I.** not happening, now this.

What else could go wrong? There was still the toilet smashing craze to contend with. It was hard to "police" the toilets for a whole gig, therefore they were prime targets for vandal-ism. By the end of each gig the ladies were flooded. Someone found it a great laugh. We sure didn't. Thankfully the toilet smashing craze didn't last very long.

Lost £210 on **Jailcell Recipes**. Lost £96 on **Babydigger**.

Drive

DUKKAH

Ingredients

1/2 cup roasted nuts (hazelnut, pistachio, etc.)

2 tbsp coriander

1/3 cup sesame seeds, lightly toasted

1 tbsp cumin seeds

1 tbsp dried thyme

salt and pepper

Preparation

1. Grind together in a mortar and pestle or food processor.

2. Eat with bread dipped in olive oil.

"Simple as that. Experiment with quantities to taste if you like, as there is no "correct" recipe as such. It's pretty good without the bread or olive oil too. This Egyptian dish is both stimulating and good for you. As such this book seems an appropriate home.

Memories of Hope gigs? The Fugazi gig in McGonagles with N.O.W. supporting, for one. Mind blowing! Or the night when Nomeansno played their first Irish gig at The New Inn and tore the roof off the sucker with elas-tic basslines, jazz-punk drums and sheets of blasting gui-tar. All with sound clear as a bell. Yesss. And many, many more . . ."

—*Chris Heaney, Lawnmowers*

ANTIC HAY + FLYING KIDNEY + BLOODY JELLIES
THE GRATTAN, OCT. 23, 1990

Gaynor from Preston was organizing a tour for Dutch band **Antic Hay** and she asked if they could add Ireland to it. They were on the same label as **Vernon Walters** and Gaynor had some good taste in music so I said fine, without hearing the band.

The Grattan was a small venue that was cheap to rent. It held up to 150 people but didn't look deserted if there were 30 there. It was perfect for local bands starting out and for touring bands that might not attract a big crowd.

As **Not Our World** were regular guests there, the manager Peter Quigley was quite receptive to any Hope gigs we wanted to put on. So we booked The Grattan and tried to encourage people to come along. Luckily it wasn't deserted, although only 27 people turned up on the night.

Antic Hay surprised me. I personally didn't like them; they reminded me of **U2**. Most of the 27 people at the gig were more impressed by **Flying Kidney**, who also played. **Flying Kidney** were preoccupied with quirkiness. Their music challenged the listener and people in Dublin at that time weren't willing to be challenged.

BREAD SANDWICH

Ingredients

One fine selection of one singular type of bread.
A carefully chosen knife. If you choose your bread carefully, you may be able to discard this "ingredient." I am told certain bakers will slice your bread into similarly sized "slices." These "slices" can be obtained from most food-shops in the form of a "pan."

Preparation

1. Get bread.
2. Hold bread firmly with left hand.
3. Make three incisions in bread with knife, until three similarly sized slices emerge from bread.
4. Place "slices" of bread atop one another such that you have a nice sandwich.
5. Eat.

Note: If you have opted for the pre-sliced variety of bread (also known as the "sliced pan"), you may skip stages 2 and 3 of my directions. Just go ahead and assemble the bread.

—Colm Bannon, Flying Kidney

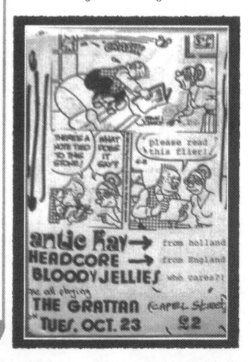

FIREWATER CREED + RENEGADE + LETHARGIC | THE ATTIC, NOV. 25, 1990 | BENEFIT FOR STOP ANIMAL EXPERIMENTS

Andrew Bass asked if I was interested in getting bands to play in The Attic. For £30 we'd get the room and a sound engineer. It sounded interesting to me but I didn't want to become a local promoter.

It has always puzzled me as to why music is so inaccessible to people who aren't old enough to drink in pubs. Most folk start off in bands when they are under 18 but there is nowhere for them, legally, to play.

Back in the late '80s, Ireland's bar-owners had a strange interpretation of the licensing laws. They would allow "minors" (under-18's) on their premises until 6:30 but only if accompanied by a legal guardian and, obviously, without serving them alcohol. The police drew a blind eye if

minors were on the premises before that time. That "law" has since been rubbished but in 1990 the only way to have no age restrictions at a gig was to play it in the afternoon. So I asked if it could happen!

The Attic's manager, Lenny, agreed to try out Sunday gigs with no age restrictions, starting at 4pm. Again, licensing laws meant people weren't legally allowed on the premises (even to set-up equipment) between 2:30 and 4pm so sound checks had to be completed by 2:30.

In response to Andrew's suggestion to me, I thought the best thing to do was to have a series of afternoon benefit gigs leading up to Christmas.

EXOTIC SPICED FRUIT SALAD WITH SYRUP

Ingredients

3 bananas
10 lychees
20 strawberries
2 kiwi fruit
8 passion fruit
1 orange
1 tbsp chopped mint
syrup
6 tbsp sugar
1 clove
1/4 tsp Chinese five spice
zest of 1 lime
zest of 1/4 lemon
1 vanilla pod split lengthways
1 tsp finely grated ginger
2 mint sprigs
1 1/2 cup water

Preparation

1. Combine syrup ingredients in a saucepan with 1 1/2 cups water.
2. Bring to the boil and stir until sugar has dissolved.
3. Remove and cool. Overnight gives a great flavor but 2 hours is sufficient.
4. Wash, peel, and chop all fruit except the passion fruit. Place in a large bowl.
5. Sieve the syrup into the bowl of fruit. Discard pod, clove, etc.
6. Cut the passion fruit in half and scoop the pulp and juice into the salad.

—*Jennifer Trouton, Belfast Gig Collective*

THERAPY? + SHRED | THE ATTIC, DEC. 2, 1990
BENEFIT FOR M.E. ASSOCIATION

I still felt ill and was seriously lacking in energy. Post viral fatigue syndrome had given way to a new diagnosis—M.E. If I took even any small exercise I suffered severe muscle pain. My parents bought me a typewriter and I got to work on doing a new fanzine (Sketch). I spent the little bit of energy I had on writing letters.

Valerie, Miriam and the Bearded Lady agreed to help organize these benefits. We arranged the bands between us and got Paddy to do up a poster.

The best way to publicize the gigs was to do a newsletter to inform people. Hence React was born. It started out as 500 2-sided photo-copied A4 pages, and cost me £20. It proved a good way of getting the word out. I put it in record shops/ book shops and cafés as well as giving it out at gigs.

I wrote React solely so I could pass on to other folk some bands I thought were good. I had heard a lot of good music from bands that weren't getting exposure anywhere. React gave me a chance to write some brief stuff about a band and people could take it or leave it after that. It also allowed Hope a chance to advertize our gigs.

React became monthly and spread to 5,000 printed copies. It fizzled out after three years. It became a chore. I was investing a lot of energy into it and it had advanced from my original intentions. People were taking things too personally. They wanted their band to be reviewed (favorably). They wanted their gig to be mentioned. My feeling on it was if they felt strongly about it they should do one them-selves. So I stopped doing it.

INNOCENT EGGS

Ingredients

mushrooms
garlic
onion
brown rice
veg stock
tofu
corn

Preparation

1. Chop up mushrooms, garlic and onion and lightly stir fry them.
2. Boil some brown rice but try and retain a crunchy texture.
3. Add some vegetable stock to the mushrooms, etc.
4. Get two large pieces of tofu and carve them in semi eliptical shapes so that they resemble eggs.
5. Scoop out tiny hollows in the tofu and fill with corn.
6. Serve the mushrooms/garlic/onions on the bed of rice, add the "comedy" eggs and garnish with a bit of basil. Voila!

"I was going to submit my own recipe for 'teeth-grinder' but I don't think it's legal!"
—Andy Cairns, Therapy?

WHIPPING BOY + HOUSE OF BYRON + GROWN UPS
THE ATTIC, DEC. 9, 1990 | BENEFIT FOR RAPE CRISIS CENTRE

The **Therapy?** gig in The Attic was absolutely packed. You could sense at this time that there was a buzz around the band. People who were rarely at gigs came out to this one. The Attic wore its title well. Situated upstairs in the small White Horse Inn it could fit 30 people comfortably and 100 people very uncomfortably.

All health and safety regulations went out the window the day **Therapy?** played there. Lenny was very worried that his pub would be closed down but still continued to serve beer. This gig, along with the other four in the series, provided something completely different from a normal Sunday afternoon in the lead up to Christmas.

The Whipping Boy played the following week and almost drew an equally good crowd. It is ironic that both **Whipping Boy** and **Therapy?** then went on to sign major label record deals. We had decided that Hope would not work with a band on a major record label. My main reason for wanting Hope to go down this road was in reaction to the way that record labels went about their business and how they were linked into other businesses (namely the arms trade). I also felt that the music business has enough people working for it and if a band subscribes to the business they have the option of utilizing that machinery.

If Hope could stay outside the machine as much as possible we could show people inside and outside bands that there was an alternative. So major label bands were turned down and not approached. It wasn't a snub or a judgement. It was just something we wished to do. It also left us open for contradiction—something people were only too willing to point out.

REG'S INDONESIAN VEG CURRY

Ingredients

well-stocked spice rack
onions, garlic, and a collection of vegetables of your choice but ideally including broccoli, cauliflower and potatoes
1 can coconut
bay leaves

Preparation

1. Heat the onions and garlic in a pan.
2. Add: 1/2 tsp of cumin, 1/2 tsp of coriander, 1/4 tsp of ginger, 1/4 tsp of chili, 1/4 tsp of paprika, 1 tsp of lemongrass, a pinch of cayenne, a pinch of nutmeg and a pinch of cinnamon.
3. Add vegetables and cook till veggies are done.
4. Add can of coconut milk.
5. For a healthy option, one may add a tablespoon of yeast extracts at this point. (Keep the B vitamins up—good old Marmite.)
6. Add 2 bay leaves. Add salt and pepper as required and serve with basmati rice.

"The ideal dish after a round of golf!!!!"
—Cormac O'Farrell, singer Grown-Ups
with help from Reg the ex-vegan

SLOTH | THE ATTIC, DEC. 16, 1990 | BENEFIT FOR VEGETARIAN SOCIETY OF IRELAND

KATHLYN MURPHY'S TOMATO AND RED BELL PEPPER SOUP

Ingredients

1 onion, peeled and chopped
4 tbsp olive oil
1 garlic clove, peeled and chopped
2 1/2 pints vegetable stock
14 oz can tomatoes
sprig thyme
1 tsp tomato paste
1/2 tsp ground cinnamon
2 red bell peppers, roasted—see below for how to do this trick!
1 tsp lime juice

Preparation

1. Heat the olive oil (medium to low heat), and cook the onion until it is transparent (10 min. approx.).
2. Add garlic for one minute.
3. Add stock, tomatoes, thyme, puree, cinnamon, salt/pepper and bring to the boil, reduce heat and simmer for 2 minutes
4. Stir in the roasted peppers
5. Purée soup in a blender and add lime to taste

Roasted Peppers

Under the grill, or even directly on the gas ring, char the peppers, turning them as soon as one area gets blackened. Yes that is right, until as much of the skin is black as possible. Transfer to bowl, and cover with plastic wrap, or else put in a plastic bag, or even a damp (clean!!!) tea cloth. Leave to cool. Then remove the skin and seeds. If they are still hot and you are in a hurry, you can peel them under the cold tap.

—*Michael Murphy, Pleasure Cell*

The five charities were picked out after discussions with Valerie, Miriam and the Bearded Lady. We could have run a gig every week for a year and still have had more than enough good causes. We decided to go with ones that meant something to us and hopefully raise interest among people who were going to the gigs.

We handed out leaflets at each gig but other than raising money I often wonder about the long term value of such events. I would rather they took place than didn't; I would rather they didn't have to take place at all.

The cynic in me suggests that they change nothing. The optimist belives that someone may relate to it, somewhere, sometime.

We raised the following amounts:

£150	ME ASSOCIATION of IRELAND
£90	RAPE CRISIS CENTRE
£108	STOP ANIMAL EXPERIMENTS
£6	VEGETARIAN SOCIETY of IRELAND
£65	IRISH SOCIETY for PRE-VENTION of CRUELTY to CHILDREN

All organizations were very grateful. This made me think about how we sometimes don't bother with things because they seem so unimportant on a wider scale. £90 to the RCC is probably loose change by their standards but they really appreciated the effort. It's the gesture, the small step that counts. Whenever I think about my small world not making a difference, I am reminded of that.

THE UMBRELLAS | THE ATTIC, DEC. 23, 1990 | BENEFIT FOR ISPCC

My musical influences in early life come from my family. I can't claim anything else. It was my brothers who turned me on to to punk, returning from their weekly expeditions to Advance Records and Golden Discs on Liffey Street.

They continued listening to punk but also moved on to other music. I was left behind, having developed a penchant for their record collection.

My brother Gar is a huge ska fan and it was with him in mind that I asked **The Umbrellas** to play. I knew their singer Barry (now in **Skint**) from the times when his previous band **Hey Presto** had played with **Not Our World**.

Up to now Gar (along with other brothers John and Joe) had helped if we needed assistance with transport, or on the night at some gigs. They were willing weight bearers of PA stacks and were always available. Gar had also been helping me with stuff due to my illness so I thought he'd like to see "The Brollies" two days before Christmas.

He enjoyed it, as did 50-odd others who forgot about their shopping for a while and supported this gig. It may seem odd criteria for selecting a band but **The Umbrellas** were a good band and one worth asking to play.

WELL-FED'S VEGGIE BURGER

Ingredients

1 medium onion
2 tbsp butter
1 tbsp mild curry powder
1 green bell pepper
2 oz mushrooms
1 tbsp soy sauce
3/4 cup red lentils
3/4 cup whole wheat breadcrumbs
4 oz peanuts
1 tbsp peanut butter

Preparation

1. Place red lentils in 2 cups of water and cook slowly for 20 minutes until water is absorbed.
2. Sauté the onions in the butter until transparent, add curry powder and cook for 1 minute. Add mushrooms and green pepper and cook for 5 minutes. Add soy sauce and set aside.
3. In a food processor or grinder blend the peanuts and breadcrumbs until fine.
4. Combine all these ingredients in a large bowl with the peanut butter.

When cooled, form into burger shapes and fry in a shallow pan.
These go great with:

TOMATO SAUCE

Ingredients

14 oz can Italian plum tomatoes
2 tablespoons olive oil
2 cloves garlic
1 medium onion
2 tbsp parsley, chopped (use basil or oregano as alternative or extra if required)

Preparation

1. Heat the oil and put in the finely chopped garlic and onion, and fry gently without browning.
2. Add the tomatoes and their juice, and cook briskly uncovered, stirring occasionally, for 20 minutes.
3. When the sauce thickens, puree in a blender or food-processor, re-heat, season, stir in the chopped parsley.

—*Joe Fahy, Luggage*

SUBURBAN REBELS + VIOLENT PHOBIA | THE ATTIC, DEC. 30, 1990

Morty was the aforementioned editor of *Sunny Days* fanzine so when he asked could his band play Dublin with another Cork band I was only too happy to be involved and to be one of the 30 people to pay in and see them.

GREEN LENTILS IN CILANTRO AND COCONUT MILK

Ingredients

- 2 cups green lentils; first boil for 8–10 min., drain and rinse
- 4 cloves garlic, finely chopped
- 1 large onion, chopped into chunky slices
- 1 good big, long red chili pepper, chopped into thin rings and keeping the seeds
- 1 red and 1 yellow bell pepper, sliced
- 1 can coconut milk (or dried coconut milk powder mixed with 2 cups of water)
- 1 lemon
- 1/2 lb long, thin, green runner beans, sliced
- 2 tbsp extra virgin olive oil
- 1/2 in. fresh ginger, finely chopped
- 1 handful fresh cilantro
- 1 generous pinch turmeric powder
- 1 generous pinch Garam Masala, or other basic curry mix powder
- 1 generous pinch marjoram

Preparation

1. Heat virgin olive oil in a frying pan.
2. Fry the onions and garlic.
3. Add the turmeric, Garam Masala (or other curry powder) and marjoram and keep frying and turning.
4. After 2 mins or so add the ginger, chilli pepper and red and yellow peppers and continue to stir. After, say, 4 more mins add cilantro—just pulling it apart with your hands as you do so, leaving nice leaf-shaped visible pieces.
5. Fry and stir for just 1 min more.
6. Remove from the heat and place in an ovenproof dish.
7. Add the coconut milk (or powdered coconut milk with water).
8. Mix the ingredients up a bit.
9. Add the ready-boiled green lentils and washed and cut green runner beans.
10. Stir more and add a little water until all the ingredients are just about covered by liquid.
11. Cover with silver foil.
12. Place in a pre-heated oven at about 400°F and leave for about 30 mins.
13. Squeeze lemon on it after removing from oven.
14. Allow to stand for 5 mins before serving.

Serving Suggestions

1. A salad of grated carrot and cucumber with a dressing of pepper, tsp of condensed orange juice and a splash of soy sauce.
2. Fluffy rice. I recommend boiling water in a pan with a lid, adding the rice, so that there is about 1/2 in of water above the rice, turning the heat down very low and replacing the lid—it can also be good to put a dish towel across the pan under the lid to allow for even more dehydration. Wait until all the water has evaporated.

—Morty McCarthy, Suburban Rebels
Sultans Of Ping

COWBOY KILLER | THE ATTIC, JAN. 19 + THE GRATTAN, JAN. 21, 1991 (W/ PARANOID VISIONS) | NCAD (LUNCH) + TRINITY COLLEGE (EVENING), JAN. 18, 1991

Through *Sketch* I came into contact with Kip Xool, the drummer of **Cowboy Killers**. They were based in Wales and really wanted to come over to Ireland. Paddy was in NCAD at the time and he got them a lunchtime gig there. I contacted Trinity College about the possibility of the band playing there also. **Senseless Things** were already booked in but they added **Cowboy Killers** to the bill.

At this point the word had spread around Dublin that Hope were the people who put **Fugazi** on and I think both colleges were secretly hoping that they could get **Fugazi** the next time they played Ireland. I never said they could, but come to think about it, I don't

remember saying they couldn't, either.

Both college gigs came with set guarantee fees, which meant **Cowboy Killers** could cover their ferry fare. We then booked another two Dublin gigs. They came over for a weekend and did a Dublin tour.

Their Attic gig nearly brought about the downfall of the floor. The place was packed and despite Lenny's frantic efforts people just wouldn't stop dancing. The plaster was coming off the ceiling below and the floor was literally shaking. Those who weren't dancing were standing on tables and seats. It was crazy. The Grattan on the following Monday evening was only slightly more refined. Very slightly.

PAELLA (WITHOUT THE FISH, UNLESS YOU WANT KNOWLEDGE)

Ingredients

2 cups rice
1 onion, coarsely cut
1 chopped tomatoes
1 clove garlic
1 handful mushrooms
green/red/yellow bell pepper, chopped
3 tbsp grated coconut
veggie stock (to boil rice in)
2 tbsp pine nuts (to taste)
1 1/2 tsp Chinese five spice
1 tsp curry powder
1 tsp cayenne pepper
1 tsp turmeric
some tofu if you want

Preparation

You will need a pan or pot with a large base (mainly for convenience).
1. Heat the oil in a pan, fry the onion.
2. Add the rice and stir in.
3. Add tomatoes and garlic.
4. Cook at moderate heat for a few minutes.
5. Add coconut, peppers and mushrooms.
6. Add nuts, spices and tofu if you wish.
7. Add stock (twice the volume of rice).
8. Bring to the boil and simmer for 15 minutes on a low heat.
9. Check if rice is cooked and presto, EAT away.

—*Michael Wheeler*

SPLINTERED | TRINITY COLLEGE, FEB. 1, 1991 (W/ CHRISTINA CALLS)
CHARLIE'S, FEB. 2, 1991 (W/ PARANOID VISIONS + GROWN-UPS)

TOFU AND RED BELL PEPPERS SZECHUAN STYLE

Ingredients

1 or 2 cloves garlic
1/2 cup chopped scallions (or onions)
1 tsp peanut butter or canola oil
2 tsp fresh chopped ginger
1 or 2 red chili peppers, finely chopped
1 red bell pepper, cut into bite-size pieces
1 block tofu, cut the way you like it
2 tsp hoisin sauce
2 to 4 tsp water
1 tsp sugar
1 tsp sesame oil or soy sauce to taste
2 tsp sesame seeds
steamed rice

Preparation

1. Fry the tofu in some hot canola oil, adding soy sauce every now and then.
2. When the tofu has turned brown and is a little crispy, leave the oil in the pan and set the tofu aside. Or you can drop that stage and just fry the tofu together with the spices. It won't get very well fried then, but it's up to you to decide how you like your tofu, right?
3. Heat up the peanut oil (not too hot) and fry the garlic, the ginger and the onions. If you like your food spicy add some chopped chili, too. If you don't feel too adventurous, take out the seeds. That will give it a little less kick. I always use scallions, because they add some nice green color to the dish, but plain old onions will do, too.
4. After about 2 minutes add the bell pepper and the hoisin sauce. (You should be able to get this at any Asian market and in most bigger stores.)
5. Then add the sugar and some water until you reach the consistency you like. Let it simmer for about 5 minutes (depending on how you like your pepper).
6. Taste it and add some soy sauce if you like. All you gotta do now is add the tofu and heat it up again.
7. Turn off the heat, add the oil and sprinkle some sesame seeds on top. You're done! Serve with steamed rice.

—*Marianne Hofstetter*

The Attic's management were tiring of the afternoon gigs with no age restrictions and a new, slightly bigger venue called Charlie's approached Hope. They said they would go with Saturday afternoon gigs and would agree to let in under-18's.

Charlie's Bar on Aungier Street was to be home to many gigs for the next nine months. Saturday afternoon seemed a better time for a gig. People go into town anyway on a Saturday. More and more people had been in contact about coming over so we tried to go with a regular no age restrictions event every fortnight in Charlie's—perfect!

Richo from *Grim Humour* fanzine was in a band called **Splintered** and they wanted to visit Ireland. We agreed on a suitable date and got a fee-paying gig in Trinity.

The **Splintered** gig was my introduction to hair crimpers. The first thing Richo requested when he got to my house (after a long car-ferry journey) was "where's the socket for my hair crimpers?"

My guitar tuner went missing after this gig. The fact that it had been a recent Christmas present made it worse. To my knowledge this was the only time something vanished at a Hope gig.

The Grownups

QUICKSAND | BOLTON ST COLLEGE (LUNCH), FEB. 23, 1991 | CHARLIE'S, FEB. 24, 1991 (W/ SLOTH) | THE GRATTAN, FEB. 26, 1991 W/ SKIN HORSES + AFFLICTED

Christy Colcord in England was a contact for many American bands who wanted to tour Europe. She heard about what we were doing through a friend of hers in Belfast and rang to ask if **Quicksand** could come over. They had released one 7" on Revelation Records and featured people who used to be in New York bands **Gorilla Biscuits** and **Youth Of Today**.

Quicksand

NUT BURGERS

Ingredients

8 oz mixed peanuts
1/2 cup whole wheat flour
3 tbsp chopped green veg
1 tbsp sunflower seeds
1/2 tsp mixed herbs
1 onion
1 grated carrot
1 tbsp parsley
2 tbsp oil
water to bind

Preparation

1. Sautée onion in hot oil. Add in grated carrot and cook until soft.
2. Mix all ingredients together in a bowl.
3. Divide into 8 burgers. Place on an oiled tray.
4. Bake for 12 minutes. Turn and bake for a further 12 minutes until brown.
5. Or fry in oil until golden brown.

—*Maureen Quinn, Saru Vegetarian Guest house, Sligo, Northwest Ireland*

No matter what bands they had been in before, we would still have put on the gig—if they were willing to travel, we were happy to give them a place to stay. However, after hearing the music of **Quicksand** we were very happy to have accommodated them.

By now Bolton Street college were offering to do gigs and Fran in Kildare asked about putting bands on Saturday evening. A band could feasibly play Charlie's in the afternoon and drive the short distance to Kildare for a gig that night. It meant a lot more work for the band but it also gave them a greater chance to cover their costs of travelling over to Ireland.

Julia and others in Belfast got the Belfast Gig Collective going so bands could travel up there on a Sunday for a gig.

There was a Thursday—Tuesday special offer on the car ferry so it proved cost effective to come over to Ireland on a Thursday night/Friday morning to play Friday lunch, Friday night, Saturday afternoon and evening, Sunday evening and finally Monday again (usually in Dublin). **Quicksand** availed themselves of this offer.

One hundred-twenty people were at the Charlie's gig—the venue wasn't packed but many, many more say they were here.

JAILCELL RECIPES + FORCE FED | CHARLIE'S, MARCH 10, 1991

Jailcell Recipe's second visit to Ireland, organized through Belfast—a bigger crowd this time, 90 people paid in to see them in Dublin.

Quicksand

THAI YELLOW PUMPKIN AND GREEN BEAN CURRY

Ingredients

20 oz can coconut milk

1-2 tsp yellow or red Thai paste depending on how hot you like it (most have fish paste in them so check)

1 tbsp sugar

3 lemongrass stalks each cut into three and bruised with the flat of a knife

3 lime leaves (if available)

1/2 tsp turmeric

2 lb pumpkin/butternut squash (if pumpkin is unavailable or not to your taste, substitute chickpeas)

1 lb green beans (snow peas, runner, french)

juice of 1/2 lime

fresh cilantro

Preparation

1. Skim the thick creamy top off the can of coconut milk into a large saucepan, add Thai paste, put over a medium heat, and with a whisk or fork, beat until combined.

2. Add remainder of coconut milk, sugar, lemongrass, lime leaves and turmeric. Bring to the boil and add the chopped pumpkin. Cook on a fast simmer until pumpkin is tender, approx. 15 minutes.

3. Add the chopped green beans. Simmer for an additional 5 minutes.

4. Just before serving add the lime juice (taste & add the other half if you feel it needs it). Sprinkle a generous amount of roughly chopped coriander on top. Serve with basmati rice.

—Jennifer Trouton, Belfast Gig Collective

PEAR AND CARDAMOM CAKE

Ingredients

9 oz (2 cups) dried pears
1 1/3 cups unsweetened apple juice
4 tsp cardamom pods
1 cup molasses
1 cup golden syrup
1/2 cup veg margarine
3 cups whole wheat all-purpose flour
1/2 tsp baking soda
1/2 tsp each ground
ginger/cinnamon/cloves
1/2 cup light muscovado sugar
4 cups medium oatmeal
1 tbsp porridge oats

Preparation

1. Boil pears in saucepan with apple juice. Remove and leave to cool.
2. Grind the cardamom pods in pestle and mortar (alternatively bash with the flat of a large knife). Discard pod, reserve the seeds.
3. Heat the molasses and margarine until marg is melted, cool.
4. Sift the flour, baking soda, ginger, cinnamon and gloves into a bowl. Stir in the sugar and oatmeal.
5. Add 1/2 the cooled pears and all the fruit juice to the bowl with the cardamom seeds and melted marg syrup mix. Stir.
6. Turn the mixture into a greased and lined square cake pan, scatter the remaining pears and oats on top. Bake in 325°F preheated oven for 1 1/4 hours until risen and a skewer inserted into the centre comes out clean. Leave to cool before removing from pan.

—Jennifer Trouton

Go!

HERB GARDEN + VILLAGE IDIOTS | CHARLIE'S, MARCH 16, 1991

The **Herb Garden** gig was a disaster. The first really bad one in Charlie's, it brought back memories of **Antic Hay** in The Grattan. I still had this plan that if Hope was put on the poster people would still go along to the gig regardless of who was playing.

We were starting to sell fanzines and records at gigs. People were being encouraged to bring out their own zines. We were trying to create a small community, one that could work together and help each other out. It all worked fine when there was a band playing that people had heard of and they actually wanted to see. It also was of additional value if the band was American. Not sure why but people appreciated American bands more.

In the case of Herb Garden 22 people paid in. Considering that the people putting on the gig paid in, that literally meant 22 people there plus band members. Emmet Greene from Cork travelled up to this gig with the **Village Idiots**. Emmet has continued to put gigs on in Cork.

BROWN SAUCE WITH EVERYTHING

It sits really nice
on a Luscious Lentil bake
When I see it on salad
my taste buds shake
When it's lovingly poured
on a golden Brown Spud
The taste is like sunshine
though it looks like mud
So save me your menu
of burgers with cheese
A bottle of Brown sauce
and I'm weak at the knees
All that I need
I can pluck from the ground
Dripped in Brown Sauce
to make it taste Sound

—*Padge Tierney, Violent Phobia*

VIOLENT PHOBIA PIZZA

Ingredients

1 pizza crust (make sure there's no dairy in it)
1 jar pasta sauce
2 medium-sized tomatoes
1 green bell pepper
1 packet button mushrooms
1 small onion
1 jar corn
1 jar pitted olives
1 block vegan cheese
1 bottle brown sauce

Preparation

1. Thinly slice the tomatoes, mushrooms and onion, chop the pepper and halve the olives.
2. Cover the pizza base with the pasta sauce and put all the veg evenly on the pizza.
3. Finely grate the vegan cheese all over the pizza and pop into the oven at about 400°F for between 10 and 15 minutes (bear in mind the cheese doesn't melt like dairy cheese—it's done when the cheese is slightly browning).
4. Remove from oven and draw a circled A on the top with the brown sauce.

*"The sauce must be the YR brand, which at the risk of appearing to be sucking corporate cock, is by far superior to the other brown sauces available. In fact it's so good I wrote a song about it for a band I was in after. **VP** called **Dole Eireann** who terrorized the west coast (mainly Galway) for a year."*

—*Padge Tierney, Violent Phobia*

AC TEMPLE | CHARLIE'S, MARCH 30, 1991

GRASSY NOEL'S MINT HUMMOUS

Ingredients

2 bulbs garlic

1 can chickpeas (or equivalent prepared and soaked overnight)

juice of 1/2 lemon

2 tbsp soy yogurt—if there is such a thing!!!!

1 tbsp tahini (sesame seed paste)

a few sprigs of mint

salt and pepper to taste

Preparation

Chuck the lot into any old container and insert the hand blender until smooth.

"Wicked with breads or alongside salads."

—*Noel, AC Temple*

It cost £70 to hire Charlie's, including a PA, sound engineer and staff. This equalled 30 people at £2.50 in and allowed us great leeway in agreeing to put bands on. The idea was to get people to see all sorts of music, once the bands were independent.

To be honest it didn't really work. There was a diversity between the bands but unfortunately people still only went to certain gigs. Despite the consistent few regulars in attendance, each band seemed to attract a specific audience. I suppose people like what they like and that's all.

AC Temple made a great racket. They weren't a straight-ahead punk/hardcore band or even an indie band. However, after this gig I felt like stopping. Hope could have just concentrated on agreeing to put on the formulaic hardcore/punk bands—but then it would have seemed like a job or service. That certainly wasn't the point.

Instead of not being involved anymore, I decided that if the band were happy to play and I was happy to be involved in putting them on, then the people who didn't show up weren't going to affect me.

It took gigs like this to make me realize that.

Go!

GORILLA BISCUITS + DRIVE + UNSOUND + ROOSEVELT'S FARM
CHARLIE'S, APRIL 16, 1991

Christy asked if New York band **Gorilla Biscuits** could play Ireland. **Drive** from England had been looking to come over on the same weekend. So we thought why not make it a double bill?

I rang Tony Doherty from NorthWest Musician's Collective in Derry, because his number was in the *Hot Press Yearbook*, and asked if they would be interested in putting on certain bands. They had a venue up there and Tony agreed with relish. Though **Gorilla Biscuits** and **Drive** didn't make it to Derry, Tony asked if **Roosevelt's Farm**, from Derry, could play Dublin so this gig seemed like an opportune time.

Gorilla Biscuits featured some people from **Quicksand** so we felt there would be a good crowd at the gig. Their ferry was due to arrive into Cork and we asked Emmet and Shane Fitzsimons to organise something there. They readily agreed as, up to now, American bands hadn't had time to play outside Dublin and Belfast. Unfortunately, **Gorilla Biscuits** missed their ferry from France and the Cork gig went ahead without them. So, £180 lost on that one.

Gorilla Biscuits made it into Dublin on time and Charlie's was packed out. The queues had formed early and the doors had to be opened during the soundchecks, as there were complaints from the adjoining businesses. We fit 200 people into Charlie's and the venue was full beyond capacity. We hadn't realized just how popular this band was—in an all too rare occurrence, people were mouthing the words along to the songs. Our plan was to try and get these to return.

TWIN TOWERS TACOS

Ingredients

1 lb tofu (extra firm)
1 can pinto, black or refried beans
1 can corn
taco shells/burrito wrappers
tomato
onion
black olives
hot sauce
1 packet taco seasoning OR make your own using 1 tsp each cayenne pepper, garlic powder, chili powder, salt and 2/3 cup water

Preparation

1. Sift the four seasoning ingredients together with a fork, if not using a pack, and then sprinkle it onto the skillet mixture. Add a small amount of water, maybe 2—3 ounces and mix well.
2. In a large skillet, mix tofu or tofu crumbles (veggie "ground round" is great) together with beans and heat until warm.
3. Add seasoning mixture
4. Add corn and stir it all up again.
5. Now that the main filling is done, stuff it into your taco shells (or burrito wrappers) and top with your favourites like tomato, onion, avocado, sprouts, black olives and hot sauce.

"Called this because we live in two identical two-story houses that are next door to each other. We developed this dinner and as a result of neighbourliness, share with our respective upstairs and downstairs neighbours."

*—Chuck Ragan, Hot Water Music
and Jessica Mills, Reina Aveja*

THE KEATONS + I AM THE WALTONS + TENSION
CHARLIE'S, APRIL 16, 1991

One month after the **Herb Garden** disaster came **The Keatons** fiasco. Twenty people came to Charlie's to see them with two other bands.

The Keatons' managed to play in Cork, with the help of Emmet, and in a new club in Dublin called the Anarchy Night Café, which at the time was based in Fibber Magees, Parnell Street.

However, given the circumstances of the Charlie's gig it just seems so irrelevant. My only memories of **The Keatons** are of my Nan dying some days before the gig. It had a devastating effect on me and even now I look back with huge fondness on the woman who plied me with chips from a very young age. She was great and I loved her. I never told her that to her face.

ROOT VEGETABLE SOUP WITH GREENS

Simple broth thickened with potato and stale bread known as pancotto in Italy.

Ingredients

olive oil
3 onions
1/2 garlic bulb
2 large floury potatoes
1 lb vegetables (whatever is in the garden ready)
1 mug water
1 cup stale bread
bunch of greens
salt and pepper
lemon juice

Preparation

1. Gently fry onions and garlic in olive oil.
2. Add potatoes and veg plus seasoning and half water.
3. Simmer 20 minutes

4. Add bread plus enough water to make broth.
5. Season.
6. Add greens.
7. Cook for 10 mins.
8. Leave for as long as possible to cool down and blend.
9. Heat up and serve with big squeeze of lemon juice and splash of olive oil.

"Genuine vegan recipes due to poverty included:
1. Fried breadcrumbs
2. Pasta with mustard
3. Mashed potatoes (no butter, marg, milk or seasoning)
4. Bunch of bananas from Skip.

Happy times. The only time I can recall a Keaton being a vegan was singer Kev in the Czech Republic. He suffered terribly. A typical meal would be a can of tomatoes in a glass with one piece of withered lettuce. That's a salad with no meat, please."

—*Steve, The Keatons*

F.U.A.L + PARANOID VISIONS + COITUS + CIUNAS | CHARLIE'S, MAY 18, 1991

RICE PILAU

Ingredients

- 2 lbs brown rice
- 1 large onion
- 3 cloves garlic (to taste)
- 3 carrots, sliced
- 1 large potato, diced pretty small
- 2 bell peppers, diced
- 8 oz mushrooms sliced (optional)
- 1 cup cooked chickpeas
- 2 tbsp whole star anis
- 1 tsp each: whole cloves, ground coriander, cumin, cinnamon, and ginger
- 1/2 tsp ground allspice
- 4 tbsp oil for frying
- salt to taste

Preparation

1. Heat the oil in a large saucepan and fry the spices for 1 minute. This helps release their flavors. Add the onion, garlic and potato and fry for 10 minutes. You may need to put in 1/2 cup of water to prevent it from sticking to the pot.
2. Add in peppers and mushrooms (optional) and sautee for 2 minutes.
3. Wash the rice, add it to the mixture and fry for a further 2 minutes. This way the rice gets coated with the oil and comes out fluffier.
4. Put hot water into the saucepan at a ratio of 2:1 to the rice. Don't worry about putting in too little rice as you can always add more during the cooking process. Stir thoroughly once, bring to the boil and simmer with the lid on for 45–55 minutes, until the rice is cooked and the liquid is absorbed. Keep an eye on it in case all the liquid evaporates too early (as explained above).
5. Serve with peanut sauce.

PEANUT SAUCE

Believe it or not, this sauce is a winner with chips or with the Rice Pilau.

Ingredients

- 1 small onion, finely diced
- 1 clove of garlic (optional)
- 1/2 tsp chili powder
- 5 tbsp soy sauce
- 1/2 jar peanut butter
- oil for frying

Preparation

1. Fry the onion and garlic (if desired) in hot oil with the chili powder until browned.
2. Stir in the peanut butter and soy sauce.
3. Gradually add hot water until the sauce has a gravy-like consistency (or however thick you want it)

—*Suzy, Warzone Belfast*

This was the first gig since the farce of no-one turning up to see **The Keatons** the previous month.

Coitus were based in England and featured Skinny, who used to be in **Paranoid Visions**. FUAL were from Belfast and were doing an Irish tour. Both bands asked to play on the same day so they were accommodated together.

Paranoid Visions also played this gig and the records show they were given £5 for their efforts. To their credit **Paranoid Visions** made nothing of this fact. They did get to play a gig with some friends.

I don't know what is worse—playing a gig and getting nothing for a gig or glaying a gig and being given a fiver.

JAM JAR JAIL + PET LAMB + GROWN-UPS + ONION BREATH FOX + PHEASANT, MAY 30, 1991 | REACT BENEFIT

Everything abut this recipe sums up **Jam Jar Jail**. Long, a lot of work and worth it in the end. They made the effort and were wild. Few people appreciated it but those who did did realized the quality.

I don't remember thanking the bands who did these two benefits. If not I apologize and am grateful they took the time out to play and support *React* for no monetary gain.

VEGAN DINNER BURRITO

Alrighty, before we start in on the main dish I'll sub-recipe the guacamole and the salsa cuz they're not always easy to get in Ireland but they are easy to make.

GUACAMOLE

Ingredients

2 or 3 avocados
2 or 3 tbsp of chopped onion
1 jalapeño pepper chopped
1 tbsp of chopped black olives
1 tbsp of chopped cilantro
1 chopped tomato
1 garlic clove minced
1/2 tsp hot sauce (maybe more)
1 tbsp eggless mayonnaise or greek style soy yogurt
1 lemon

Preparation

1. Holding back on the avocados mix everything else into a bowl. Squeeze 1/2 lemon into the mix and throw in a couple drops of vinegar while yer at it.
2. Next mash the avocados and then add them to the mix till the whole thing is green and hangs together.
3. Lastly, squeeze the other half of the lemon on top, don't drown it but enough to cover it. This stops it from turning brown. Then put some wrap over the bowl and leave it in the fridge to chill.

SALSA

Ingredients

1 can tomato paste
1 or 2 large tomatoes
2 or 3 tbsp chopped onion
1/2 tbsp vinegar or cider vinegar
1 chopped jalapeño pepper
1/2 chopped green chili pepper
1/2 each green and red bell pepper chopped
1 tbsp chopped cilantro
1 tbsp corn

Preparation

This is easy. Throw everything into a bowl and mix it together. Then keep it chilled in the fridge till it's needed. Both guacamole and salsa share similar ingredients but the difference is that you want the guacamole to be smooth and creamy while the salsa should be crunchy and hotter tasting. Amounts and ingredients can be experimented with but if I was to say anything it wouldn't be about the peppers but the cilantro. It has a very distinctive taste and although it's a central ingredient in Mexican cuisine too much of it can make a meal taste like a weird aftershave. OK, on with the burrito.

VEGAN DINNER BURRITO, CONT.

Ingredients

1/2 lb block tofu, cubed
flour tortillas (12" or bigger)
16-ounce can refried beans
1/2 cup salsa
1/2 cup guacamole
1 medium size chopped broccoli
1 cup shredded vegan cheese
1/4 cup sunflower seeds, hulled
1/4 tsp black pepper
2 garlic cloves minced
1/4 cup chopped green onion
1/4 cup chopped regular onion
1 tbsp cooking oil
1 tbsp teriyaki sauce

Preparation

1. In a large frying pan add the tofu into hot oil.
2. In a separate pot, heat up the refried beans. If you have trouble finding a can of these just boil up a batch of pinto or black beans, mash them when they're soft and add some tomato paste to make them stick together smoothly. You can also add some salsa in with the beans at this stage as it adds more moisture to the mix and stops it sticking to the pot as much.
3. Back to the frying pan. Keep turning the cubes over with a spatula, getting them brown on all sides. Before they're finally done add the green onion, onion, garlic and black pepper. Don't put them in too soon or they'll burn before the tofu is ready.
4. In the other pot, add the broccoli once the beans start to heat up. This can be done at the last minute as the idea is not to cook the c rap out of it but keep all the good stuff intact. Also add the sunflower seeds.
5. When the tofu is just about ready give it a lash with the teriyaki sauce (if you can get one of the good ones with sake in it all the better) on the pan. The whole thing will hiss and bubble but keep turning the tofu till the cubes are completely covered with it. Then kill the heat and put a lid over it.
6. Same with the beans—when they're hot enough, kill the heat and cover.
7. Next the tortillas. If you're using a gas cooker turn on one of the plates. Drape the tortilla over it a couple of times, turning to both sides. Get it hot and a little crispy but be careful not to set it on fire or make it so crisp so that it's stiff and you can't roll it up. If you don't have a gas cooker heat up a frying pan (no oil) and turn the tortilla over on it a couple of times till again it's heated up (if you go oow!oow! as you lift it off the pan or plate then that's usually about right).
8. The finishing bits: With the tortillas lying flat, add some cheese, guacamole and salsa to the middle of each of them.
9. Next add the beans and tofu on top of that. Then pull two sides of the tortilla (east and west) over the middle and finally roll the rest of the tortilla up from the bottom till you've got a tube of flour with hot stuff inside it.
10. Alternative ingredients include rice, chopped lettuce, sprouts etc.—basically anything you can combo with beans.
11. Serve with salsa and tortilla chips to dip and munch.

—*Shane O Reilly, Jam Jar Jail*

NOFX + GO! + DECLINE | CHARLIE'S, JUNE 1, 1991
NOFX + GUMPH + AFFLICTED + FAR SIDE | FOX, JUNE 3, 1991

GAZPACHO

Ingredients

1 clump of celery
1 large onion
1 cucumber
about 15 radishes
2 avocados
3 large tomatoes
1 bell pepper
2 cans vegetable broth
4–8 cups tomato juice (or V8)
heaps of tabasco sauce

Preparation

1. Finely chop the vegetables and put in large bowl.
2. Add tabasco.
3. Pour in chilled vegetable broth and tomato juice.
4. Add tabasco sauce.
5. Chill for 1 hour and serve in a bowl of tabasco (optional).
6. That's right, no heating or cooking, it's supposed to be cold.

"What's nice about cooking gazpacho is that you don't have to cook gazpacho. This is all you gotta do. Delicious served as an appetizer, or with a vodka chaser.

Warning: no dating after consumption, breath will stink and high probability of flatulence (does not apply to Europeans)."

—Fat Mike, NOFX

Again a case of two tours happening simultaneously and of us not wanting to say no. Go! from New York were an outspoken hardcore band that tackled many issues, including homosexuality and discrimination. They wanted to come over with **Decline** from England.

NOFX, on the other hand, wanted to do a few gigs in Ireland as part of their European tour. The band made a living through their music, which poked fun at everyone. Getting the two bands on the same bill would provide them with an excellent opportunity to confront each other—a far better forum than discussing it through the letters page of big American fanzines like *Maximum Rock'n'Roll*.

This is something that is very common throughout the whole of the punk/hardcore community. People find it easy to complain in letters pages about the actions of others. We thought it would be interesting to see what would happen on the day (and make for a pretty good gig).

Nothing did happen on the day except the 140 people at the gig seemed to enjoy themselves and **NOFX** then played in the Fox and Pheasant on the Monday evening. **Go!** and **Decline** were only over for two days so they missed the Monday gig.

The gig on the Monday evening was equally insane with all four bands playing a diverse sound. It was announced on the Saturday afternoon that **NOFX** would be playing a surprise gig. I think the only surprise for people was that **Go!** weren't also playing.

NOFX

INSIDE OUT + IN MOTION + MEXICAN PETS | CHARLIE'S, JUNE 22, 1991

Ian from Meantime Records was organizing a tour for American band **Inside Out**. They were an all-female band and they seemed interesting so it was great to be able to say they could play in Dublin.

In June 1991 it was rare to have women in bands in Dublin. If **Inside Out** could be used as an influence for more women to get involved then great.

Doing the main organizing of Hope gigs at this stage were four people—two men and two women. Quite a few women went to the gigs but it seemed they played a less active role (if doing more than listening makes one more active, of course). Unfortunately, this is something that hasn't changed too much. **Mexican Pets** had a woman who played guitar and wrote songs, so hopefully Jill proved influential for others.

A question often asked has been why women aren't more involved in music. Normally I pay no attention to the gender balance of a band but faced with an all-women line up it gets me thinking as to why more men are involved. I really don't know and I hope that we never discriminated at our gigs for whatever reason.

SHEPHERD'S PIE

Ingredients

2 chopped onions
4 cloves garlic, chopped
4 tbsp olive oil
1 lb Sosmix or fake mince of your choice (or 1 lb Gimme Lean fake meat for our American friends)
3 heaped tbsp cornstarch or flour
1/2 pint veg stock
2 tbsp tomato paste
1/2 tsp Marmite (optional)
salt and pepper
1/2 bag frozen peas
7–8 mushrooms
3–4 carrots
enough mashed potatoes to cover the pie—about 5–6 spuds usually does the trick

Preparation

1. Preheat cooker to 350°F.
2. Fry onions and garlic in oil 'til soft, add Sosmix/fake mince, stir until brown.
3. In a measuring jug, mix flour with half of the stock until smooth.
4. Add the tomato paste, Marmite, and the rest of the stock. Pour over the meat & onion mixture
5. Add salt and pepper to your liking.
6. Cover and simmer for 10 minutes.
7. Pour into an ovenproof dish and stir in carrots, mushies, peas and top with the mash.
8. Bake for 1 hour.

—*Jill Hahn, Mexican Pets*

ECONOCHRIST + WORLD OF DRUMS + JAM JAR JAIL
ECONOCHRIST + GROWN-UPS + CIUNAS
CHARLIE'S, JULY 13, 1991 | FOX + PHEASANT, JULY 15, 1991

BEAN AND VEGETABLE STEW

Ingredients

1 large onion, finely chopped
1 clove garlic, finely chopped
1 green bell pepper
1 red bell pepper
1 large eggplant
1 zucchini
fresh or canned tomatoes
string beans (canned or pre-cooked)
salt and pepper to taste
plenty of olive oil

Preparation

1. Wash the eggplant, slice it open, indent the flesh, pour salt into the wounds (you know you want to), and leave aside for twenty-five mins to let it breathe/soften.

2. Place a large saucepan on low heat, coat base with olive oil, and allow it to warm through. Add onion to the pan.

3. Leave for five minutes, without allowing the onion to brown, and add the garlic.

4. After another five, add the washed de-seeded green pepper. You might want to turn the heat up slightly at this point. Leave for five, and add the red bell pepper.

5. Rinse the eggplant, wash out the salt, chop into bite-size pieces and add to the pan, along with lashings of olive oil. The more oil you add, the softer they seem to get, so it's your call on this. Wait another five minutes and guess what: it's zucchini time!

6. You can use green or yellow, just wash 'em and chop 'em up pretty small After leaving the mixture for another, yes, five minutes, add your fresh or tinned tomatoes; one can or equivalent.

7. At this point you should also add your beans, slightly less than one can or however much looks good to your eyes. Just remember they MUST be cooked already. Otherwise, say hello to a seriously upset stomach.

8. Leave this mixture to simmer away for ten to fifteen minutes, until zucchinis are soft and eggplants have gone slightly brown. This stew goes well with simple green salad, fresh bread, baked potatoes, chili-fried potatoes or on its own. It also keeps well, and can be eaten up to a couple of days after.

"The key to this dish is not to stir the ingredients too much. Just add 'em one by one, toss 'em around the pan, and let the flavours blend into each other."

—*Lee Casey, World Of Drums*

I had a bedsit that I gave over to bands when they were visiting. The neighbors never complained but I'm sure they wondered.

I was away for the **Econochrist** tour. There was a mix-up over their Derry gig. It was cancelled but they traveled up from Dublin not realizing.

I don't know whether they were annoyed or not but they decided not to tidy anything up after themselves in my small cell. When I got home, one week later, there were things growing in my pots. Awful.

BABES IN TOYLAND + PET LAMB / BABES IN TOYLAND + IN MOTION
CHARLIE'S, JULY 20, 1991 | FOX + PHEASANT, JULY 22, 1991

This was the twelfth Saturday afternoon gig of the year in Charlie's. Southern Studios had been in touch about **Babes In Toyland** playing. They were going to play Belfast and Cork with **Therapy?** and wanted to fit in the capital while they were over. I was delighted because John Loder was involved in Southern. John was involved with **Crass** and **Flux Of Pink Indians** and also helped out with Ian MacKaye from **Fugazi**.

This was a great gig and NO, **Therapy?** did not play the Dublin gig. There was confusion before this gig as the rumor spread that the **Babes** had signed to a major label. Given our refusal to deal with bands on major labels it may have seemed contradictory to put on a band just because of a link with John Loder. However, we were told they were not on a major when they visited Ireland and that's all the reassurance we needed. They subsequently signed to (and got dropped from) a major but when they played Ireland they were aligned with Southern.

It may seem a small and inconsequential point but it was important to Hope. As mentioned, Hope didn't want to be part of the major record label's machinery for their bands. We had NO guest list at our gigs, we treated all bands the same, the same way we treated people who paid in to the gigs, and anyone involved in helping with a gig paid in. This way there was no "them" and "us." For us to put on a band tied in to a major record label would have been a sign of support for the band, something we didn't want to do through our gigs, regardless of individual feelings.

Monday night and the **Babes** played the Fox. Another surprise gig, my surprise being when I was asked for ALL the money (£300) from the gig to go the **Babes**. "I think they deserve it after tonight's show, don't you?" I was too busy dreaming of those **Crass** records and thinking "this isn't right" to give the reply I wanted to.

BORSCH

Ingredients

- 4 beets (cooked)
- 2 carrots (grated)
- 2 celery stalks with leaves (chopped)
- 1 cup chopped cabbage
- 1 onion
- 2 tbsp olive oil
- 4 cups dissolved vegetable stock
- 1 tbsp red wine vinegar
- 1/2 cup tomato juice

Preparation

1. Chop the onion and sauté in a deep saucepan with olive oil.
2. Add the chopped vegetables and fry for 3 minutes approx.
3. Pour in vegetable stock, vinegar and tomato juice.
4. Cook for another 3 minutes until the vegetables are tender. Cool slightly, then serve and enjoy.

—*Dylan, Pet Lamb*

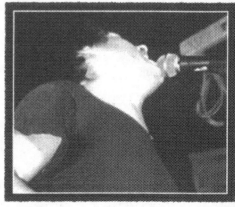

NOFX

HEADCLEANER + GROWN-UPS + PIG IGNORANCE
FOX + PHEASANT, AUG. 5, 1991

"It was with a little nervousness that I approached my first-ever Hope gig in September of 1989. The worry stemmed from

KATHY MURPHY'S TOMATO, CELERY AND APPLE SOUP

Ingredients

1 large onion, diced
5 stalks celery, chopped
1 large cooking apple, sliced
2 tbsp olive oil
3 14 oz cans chopped tomatoes
1 cup vegetable stock

Preparation

1. In the pan, cook the onion, celery and apple in the olive oil on low heat for 10 minutes.
2. Add the tomatoes and vegetable stock, and a pinch of salt and pepper, and even a teaspoon of sugar if you like (it cuts down on the acid in the tomatoes, but is not strictly necessary).
3. Bring to the boil, then reduce heat and simmer for 20 minutes.
4. Puree in the blender (it is still good if you have no blender).
5. Reheat when you are hungry for delicious soup.

"My mother is the best cook I know, and she makes a ton of great tasting vegan and vegetarian recipes. There is never a rumbling belly no matter how many people are in her home."

—Michael Murphy, The Pleasure Cell

the fact that this was in my mind a punk gig and until then my only experiences of punks was a head butt from one called Sid on a Saturday night in my teenage years that left me sprawled on the ground and various other taunts and threats from them around the Grafton Street area as I was out with my friends on Saturday afternoons, although maybe I deserved it from my rather pathetic half-Goth half—child of John Cale look that I sported.

The gig in question was **Fugazi**, whose fans did not worry me in the slightest, and **Snuff**, whose fans worried me a great deal, as at the time, in my mind, they had quite a skinhead following and after what the punks had done to me I certainly felt entitled to worry about what havoc they might achieve. Thankfully, on the way there I found out that **Snuff** had cancelled and all fear subsided, and then to make matters better Guy from **Fugazi** stopped me along the way and he asked me where the nearest phone box was. This encounter left me feeling all awestruck and I then went and took my place at the back of the venue, just in case some irate **Snuff** fans had entered and were ready to vent their anger. **The Slowest Clock**, at the time Dublin's answer to **Sonic Youth**, started the night in an angular manner and good as they were the anticipation for **Fugazi** was too much for them to be fully appreciated. All expectations for the headliners were realised complete with shaking sound system, which at one stage seemed about to topple into the audience.

After that acquaintance with Hope there was many more happy nights to be had in their company, always greeted by Niall at the door saying "Two pound please!" What a bargain that was. **Gorilla Biscuits**, double headliner of **Circus Lupus** and **Lungfish**, **Neurosis** and **Down By Law** were all highlights although there wasn't really any nights that were letdowns.

The worst part of it all was that they stopped doing it."

—JD

NOMEANSNO + PET LAMB + TENSION | MCGONAGLES, SEPT. 15, 1991

Nik Evans got in touch to say that **Nomeansno** were looking to come back to Ireland. After **Fugazi**'s success in the venue, McGonagles seemed like the perfect place. We hired it and asked **Pet Lamb** and **Tension** to play.

Paddy and Fergus were happy to help out and added to the ranks for this gig. They had gotten tired of doing regular gigs but a bigger venue requires more planning and therefore more people. For bands like **Nomeansno** (bands they enjoyed) they were happy to be involved, which was great.

I was a bit trepidatious hiring McGonagles. I'm like that before every gig. I wonder if enough people will come. **Nomeansno** had packed out the New Inn previously but that was with four other bands playing that night plus it had been a benefit. Would people want to see them again? My fears proved unfounded and McGonagles became a sauna for the evening.

It was nice to see Irish bands getting a chance to play to good crowds and with the backing of a good sound system. Doubly nice to see that they took to the occasion remarkably well and provided people with a night's entertainment.

Around this time I had the idea of starting a record label to act as a platform for Dublin based bands and provide them with a forum. Dublin had many good bands so it seemed like a good idea to document it I went in feet first. However I would not have got into it any deeper if I had realized the work ahead.

The Pleasure Cell's omission from any charting of Irish music is a crying shame. "A statement is a weapon in an empty hand" was a line from from their *New Age* 7" released independently in 1987 on their own Common Ground Records.

When the idea of a record came about it seemed like a natural honour to have reference to the **Pleasure Cell** song. I thought releasing a compilation 12" would be better than an album. We could do a series of compilations with four bands at a time. Releasing one compilation album would have involved trying to get too many bands to record stuff at the one time.

When it came to picking bands I just asked four but had planned to get many more involved afterwards. The first four that were asked were all people that had been involved for a while and were always willing to play gigs when asked. It was a way of saying thanks to them. So **In Motion**, **Ciunas**, **Mexican Pets** and **Wheel** appeared on the *Statement* 12".

I asked Sean and Ben from Rugger Bugger records what they had done to bring out their records. They were of invaluable assistance. They contacted the pressing plant and arranged for all the artwork to be printed and for the records to be shipped over. Borderline Records in Dublin accepted delivery.

It took a while for it all to come together and many arguments ensued. Some of the arguments got a little personal and I didn't enjoy the experience. However when the records came back from England, I didn't worry that Michael had loaned money to the label, or that £450 was taken from the Hope fund to get it out. I was thrilled. We had finally achieved it.

There was no launch gig. Each band got 25 copies of the record and it kind of fizzled out. If I had to do it again (and with the benefit of hindsight) things would be different. However it was 1992 and too much (too much being a little amount of effort) was expected from all parties.

SINK + AIM + STIGMATAMARTYR | CHARLIE'S, SEPT. 30, 1991

ROAST PEPPERS WITH FENNEL

Ingredients

2 large red bell peppers
1 medium fennel bulb (finoc-chio)
3–4 tomatoes
olive oil
ground coriander
a lemon

Preparation

1. Cut each pepper in half lengthways and remove seeds.
2. Place peppers in an oven-proof dish.
3. Quarter the tomatoes and place in the pepper halves.
4. Cut the fennel bulb into 8 pieces, keeping layers attached to root ends.
5. Blanch in boiling water for 5 minutes, then drain and arrange over the peppers.
6. Drizzle generously with olive oil and sprinkle with fresh pepper and a teaspoon of coriander.
7. Bake for almost an hour. When tinged with brown, remove from oven and squeeze juice from half a lemon over.
8. Serve with roast potatoes, broccoli and a wedge of lemon.

—*Colm Fitzpatrick, I Am The Waltons*

Sink came over to Ireland for a week's holiday and stayed in (what my brother kindly called) Gracepark Dump (i.e., my bedsit).

They were refreshing. They took their music from country and pop, which made a change. Considering that they featured a member of the band **The Stupids**, who were a full-on fast hardcore band, it was a challenge to the crowd.

The Charlie's gig had a good attendance and **Sink** were one of the most appreciative of bands. They played Bolton Street, Cork, Belfast and Charlie's as well as a lot of football in the park near my house.

Sink (top), Sparkmarker (bottom)

ANHREFN + NEGU GORRIAK | CHARLIE'S, OCT. 5, 1991

Negu Gorriak also stayed in the "Dumps." They were from the Basque region and couldn't speak a word of English. They didn't want to keep their gear in the van and so we filled the whole room up with equipment. I've no idea where they slept—it must literally have been ON their amps.

Unfortunately, they stayed over the day the landlord came to collect the rent and I wasn't going to be there. I left the money in an envelope, stuck it to the outside of the door with a note for the landlord. Needless to say that made him more intrigued and in he came. He found a room full of musical equipment, one Basque national with no English and NO explanation.

He had plenty of questions in the following weeks. My long-lost misunderstood Basque friends, I explained.

CREAMY COCONUT CURRY WITH ZUCCHINI AND POTATOS

Ingredients

2 tsp margarine or veg ghee
2 tsp cumin seeds
1 tsp chopped garlic
1 tsp chopped ginger
1 onion, chopped
chopped chilis, according to taste
1 cinnamon stick or 1 tsp of cinnamon powder
2 tsp curry paste or 4 tsp curry powder
2 zucchini (courgettes), cut into generously sized pieces
3 handfuls of chopped potatoes (the smaller you cut them, the sooner they will be done)
half a cup of coconut milk
sugar and salt to taste

Preparation

1. Heat up the ghee or the margarine and add all the ingredients up to the curry paste and fry for about 2 or 3 minutes. I suggest you get yourself some mild Madras Curry Paste in a jar. You'll find that in any Asian market and most supermarkets (or your local friendly Food Co-op if there is one—if there's not, well what can you do about that? — Ed). I always use mild and then kick it up with some chilis. I just like to have some red in my dish, it looks nice. You could also use dried chilis and break them up. Or buy some spicy curry paste, whatever. If you don't have any of that fabulous paste, use a generous amount of plain old curry powder, that will do, too.

2. After a few minutes, add the curry paste or powder and fry another minute.

3. Then add the potatoes and the zucchini.

4. Fry some more, stirring frequently, then add the coconut milk. Let simmer until the potatoes are done (15 to 20 minutes). You might need to add some water, if you think the dish is too thick.

5. Then add some salt and sugar until it tastes good to you.

6. You're done. Serve with rice and Indian bread.

—*Marianne Hofstetter*

SONS OF ISHMAEL + TURTLE ASSASINS + ARNHEIM
FOX + PHEASANT | OCT. 11, 1991

SURVIVOR'S PIE

If you're stranded on a desert island or England and can't find anything decent to eat try this potentially life saving recipe handed down from the surviving members of 2000 Dirty Squatters.

Ingredients + Preparation

1. Take a hubcap or snare drum with one of the heads punched out and sanitize with a liberal dousing of beer, Jaegermeister, gasoline, or lighter fluid.

2. Next, add whatever you have in the way of food lying around—bread crusts, potato peelings, space cake, cheese, etc. Add whatever water happens to be nearby (if you can't afford to buy water you can substitute beer, Jaegermeister, bong water, or in extreme situations, urine).

3. Mix these ingredients together with a knife, drum stick or fingers and place over a heat source like a campfire, hot-knife burner, or engine block. Heat for 20 minutes or until all remaining proteins are burned off.

4. Finally garnish with ketchup, mustard, or Taco Bell hot sauce packets and you've got a meal that'll keeping you going till the next squat.

—*Chris Black, Sons Of Ishmael*

Sons Of Ishmael came all the way from Canada for their Irish tour.

I was still ill with M.E. and had to take plenty of rest. I missed this gig due to that but met up with the band earlier in the day and showed them around Dublin.

Since they played I have struck up a friendship with Chris Black from **Sons Of Ishmael**. It is one of a number of friendships that have spawned from being involved with Hope.

As an aside, and as an example of how the world is such a small place, a woman wrote to me after picking up *React* on a trip to Dublin. We corresponded with each other and when Miriam and I went to Canada we stayed with this woman, our new friend.

It turned out that she was seeing Chris Black from **Sons Of Ishmael**. We talked about punk rock in Ireland and Chris had many good memories of his European tour. After the band split he ran Raw Energy Records in Toronto for a while. I believe he hasn't needed Survivor's Pie in a few years.

Back to the gig, **Turtle Assassins** came down from Derry for the night. Tony Doherty had been putting stuff on in that city and when he asked could some friends of his play in Dublin, of course we agreed.

SLUM TURKEYS + IN MOTION
SLUM TURKEY'S + MEXICAN PETS
CHARLIE'S, OCT. 19, 1991 | BARNSTORMER'S, OCT. 25, 1991

Paul Morley sang in **Slum Turkeys** and also put on gigs in his hometown, Manchester. When John Robb told him about Ireland he was straight on the phone to me. We are still friends to this day and now share tales of parenting rather than punk rock. For this trip though, Paul left his child for a few days to come over to Ireland and play.

Struck by his enthusiasm I tried to get **Slum Turkeys** as many gigs as possible. I really like their music and felt that if they were from the US they would have received a lot more recognition. **Slum Turkeys,** along with compatriots **Nerve Rack** and **Crane,** were marvelous, but completely underrated bands.

We managed to get gigs in Cork, Belfast, Derry and Arklow sandwiched in between two Dublin gigs and a lunchtime jaunt in Trinity College. The band loved being busy and wanted to just play and play.

After the tour I was struck by how appreciative the band were. A lot of bands didn't express how they felt about being over in Ireland. **Slum Turkeys** were completely different. They appreciated that someone put the effort in to get them to come and play. That attitude was reciprocated, as I was more than happy to do anything (within reason) for the band.

Some people in bands may find it hard to articulate their feelings. I appreciate that. I have

CARROT TART

Ingredients

12-14 oz carrots (about 3 large ones), grated
the same of onions (3 medium/2 large), finely chopped
1/4 cup marg or a good slosh of olive oil
pinch of thyme
2 tbsp flour
1 tsp Marmite or other yeast extract
salt and pepper

Preparation

1. Cook onions in oil/marg until soft and transparent.
2. Add carrots and thyme, cook gently, stirring often, for about 10-12 minutes.
3. Add flour, yeast extract and salt and pepper as required, stir well. cook for a few minutes more stirring all the time. Cool.
4. Line a pie or flan can with pastry and fill with the carrot mixture.
5. Heat oven to 400°F and cook pie for about 20–30 minutes. If preferred you can put a lid on (pastry obviously!) If so, seal edges and slash top of pie to allow steam to escape.

—*Kirsten Beechofer, Slum Turkeys*

always appreciated **Slum Turkeys** keeping in touch since those gigs and still being happy to get to Ireland.

PITCHSHIFTER + JAM JAR JAIL + DUST REVOLUTION
FOX + PHEASANT, OCT. 31, 1991

Pitchshifter from Nottingham asked through their friend Stuart if they could come over. It was Halloween and we managed to get them a gig at the NCAD Halloween ball as well as one in the Fox. Two gigs in the one evening would help pay their ferry fare.

They arrived at the Fox complete with TV screen and video. This portrayed some disturbing images throughout their set. A precursor to **U2**'s Zoo TV!

Unfortunately for the band, the art students of NCAD must have wanted to watch MTV and they broke the TV screen that evening. Maybe it was some sort of art statement. Understandably, **Pitchshifter** were very annoyed.

Also playing in the Fox that evening were **Dust Revolution**. None of us knew anything about the band beforehand. Shane from **Jam Jar Jail** asked if they could play. He knew the band. They didn't get too many gigs as they were on day release from Grangegorman mental institution. After their set they went around the audience almost individually looking for feedback. For that night they had stars in their eyes.

ROASTED EGGPLANTS

Ingredients

9 eggplants/aubergines cut into thick slices (1/2 in)
6 tbsp olive oil
3 garlic cloves, minced
1 tbsp red wine vinegar
1/4 tsp red pepper flakes
2 tbsp chopped fresh parsley
salt and pepper

Preparation

1. Brush the slices with 4 tbsp. of olive oil.
2. Season with salt and pepper.
3. Arrange the eggplant slices on a baking sheet, in a single layer.
4. Bake to the top rack of a 400°F oven, turning occasionally, until golden on both sides, about 15 minutes.
5. Meanwhile, in a small bowl, stir together the garlic, the remaining 2 tbsp. of olive oil and the vinegar
6. Place the eggplants in a serving platter and drizzle the garlic-oil mixture over the top.
7. Sprinkle with the red pepper flakes and parsley and serve

—*PIM, Pitchshifter*

THE EX + DOG FACED HERMANS | FOX + PHEASANT, NOV. 5, 1991

The Ex were a band whose records I listened to more than any others. I couldn't hold back my excitement when Gaynor inquired about them coming over for one day with **Dog Faced Hermans**. They were amazing and **The Ex** also played a gig afterwards as part of Bolton Street Rag week.

MIXED VEG NOODLES

Ingredients

7 cups vegetable stock

4–5 oz fresh green beans

2 handfuls mushrooms (shitake, or whatever you can afford)

6 tbs veg oil

1 large onion

1/2 lb noodles (Chinese lo mein or Japanese buckwheat soba or udon)

2 tbsp hot green chilis

4 tbsp Japanese rice vinegar

1/2 cup soy sauce (tamari or shoyu)

1/2 cup roasted or fried peanuts

2 cups bean sprouts

demerara sugar

chunk of fresh ginger

cupful fresh cilantro

3 cloves garlic

Preparation

1. Fry chopped onion really slowly in veg oil in a large soup pan for 15 minutes till they are sweet and transparent.

2. Add green beans mushrooms and any other vegetable you like and pour in vegetable stock. You can make your own if you have hours of free time like most thrash rockers do or else use two vegetable stock cubes.

3. Cover the pan and let it bubble for 1/2 hour. . .

The rest of the ingredients should be put in 6 little separate bowls in the following combinations:

1. Finely chopped chillies and rice vinegar

2. Finely chopped cilantro

3. Grated ginger, crushed garlic and soy sauce

4. Fried peanuts. Best to fry them in a frying pan slowly without oil until they go brown but not black. Then put the peanuts in a blender and grind them.

5. Bean sprouts

6. Demerara sugar

Put all these bowls of of flavorings in the middle of the table . . . The noodles should be cooked last when everything else is almost ready. Then put a wee pile of cooked noodles in each person's soup bowl. Pour the soup on top and let them spice up their own soup with the wee bowls of flavorings. Don't be stingy with the soy sauce and peanuts as they are the main flavorings. You won't believe your taste buds. Serves 6.

—*Andy Moor, The Ex*

GREEN DAY + DOG DAY | THE ATTIC, DEC. 18, 1991

GINGER TOFU

Ingredients:

1 tbsp olive oil
1 clove garlic
1 small nodule ginger
1 leek
4 sticks celery
2/3 cup veg stock
9 oz tofu
fresh parsley
salt and black pepper
finely chopped scallions

Preparation

1. Lightly fry the tofu in olive oil in a deep pan for 5 minutes or so. Remove and place aside.
2. Gently fry the onion, garlic & ginger (all finely chopped) for 10 minutes or until lightly browned.
3. Add the leak, celery and re-introduce the tofu.
4. Fry for a further 5 minutes.
5. Next add the veg stock & finely chopped fresh parsley.
6. Add salt and pepper to taste. Simmer for 15 minutes.
7. Add the scallions shortly before serving.

"Best served with noodles; rice or pasta would also be suitable accompaniments."

—Shane McGrath, Dog Day, Shred, Joan Of Arse, Not Our World

Yeah, yeah, it's all true. **Green Day** played in the Attic. It was a wintry Sunday afternoon. They used my bass, they covered up my **Sink** stickers. They took off their trousers and 40 people saw it all.

Retrospectively when people talk to me about Hope they mention **Green Day**, **Fugazi** and **Nomeansno**. If all the people who say they saw **Green Day** when they played with **Dog Day** in The Attic were actually there then the already unsteady floor in the venue would definitely have collapsed. On the day we lost £50 and the floor was perfectly safe. It's kind of novel to be able to say that they played but I would much prefer if I was able to give you a recipe from the band.

Dublin wasn't really the party city and **Green Day** left for Belfast straight after the gig, but not before getting some directions and food. They had enjoyed themselves so much in Belfast the previous night that they wanted to get back as quickly as possible.

1991 ended for Hope with this gig. We had directly put on 29 gigs. We had been involved with other gigs in Cork, Belfast, Trinity, NCAD, and Kill. People from other counties in Ireland were starting to ask about putting on gigs (they either got the address from *React* or traveled up to Dublin for a gig). *React* was up to 5,000 copies (I even find that hard to believe looking back) and there was an endless supply of bands looking to play. Being careful not to get carried away, **Green Day** put a sense of perspective on it. 40 people.

SLUNK IRISH TOUR JAN. 1992
(W/ TENSION) | ANARCHY NIGHT CAFÉ, JAN. 20, 1992
(W/ ONION BREATH + ARNHEIM) | FOX + PHEASANT, JAN. 24, 1992

Slunk wrote to me and asked about coming over. They were really persistent and I admired their ethic. They just wanted to play music and see as many places as possible. A record shop in Arklow, Co Wicklow had been taking copies of *React* and James, the manager of the shop, said he could get a venue to put on gigs there.

He asked if there were any bands interested in travelling to Arklow. I immediately passed the word on to **Slunk** and they were very keen. **Anhrefn** were also coming over to do some gigs in Belfast and Cork (they had made their own contacts since their first trip to Ireland) so they played Arklow on the night as well.

The Dew Drop Inn in Kill were unwilling to do more gigs and the person who was doing all the work there was tiring of it. Hence Arklow became the new Kill. About an hour's drive from Dublin, it was possible to get bands to play in the city on Saturday afternoon and then, circumstances allowing, head down for another gig that evening. Unfortunately, Charlie's lost interest in afternoon gigs and the manager decided to renovate the bar and to stop gigs for a while.

Slunk also got to play in the Anarchy Night Café with **Tension**. The people running the club were more than willing to allow a travelling band to play on the night. They paid whatever they could afford at the end of the evening.

Slunk's tour was rounded off by a gig in Bolton Street and trips to Cork and Belfast as well as an appearance at the Fox and Pheasant—six gigs in six days.

SMOKED TOMATO PATE

Ingredients

4 oz Port Yannock Semi Sun Dried Tomatoes
1 1/2 cups pumpkin seeds
3/4 cup cooked red kidney beans
2 cloves garlic
2 chilis diced (depending on preferred hotness)
1/2 cup olive oil
4 tbsp sunflower oil
2 tbsp toasted sesame seeds
2 lemons
sage leaves
1/4 tsp cocoa powder
2 tbsp soy sauce
1 tbsp balsamic vinegar
salt and pepper to taste

Preparation

1. Soak and cook beans (if not bought precooked).
2. Sautée garlic and chilli in sunflower oil
3. Add pumpkin seeds and continue frying, stirring constantly until seeds expand.
4. Sprinkle with sage and cocoa and turn off.
5. Liquidize balsamic, lemon, oil and seeds together.
6. Add cooked beans and tomatoes.
7. Season with salt and pepper if required or slightly more lemon juice.
8. Chill and serve with fresh salad or toasted on bread.

"This can be kept for 1 week in a fridge."
—*Phoenix Veggie Accommodation, Inch Co Kerry*

DECADENCE WITHIN + ALUMNI FEEDBACK + WORLD OF DRUMS
FOX + PHEASANT, FEB. 23, 1992
NESSUN DORMA + ZYGOTE | THE GRATTAN, MAR. 8, 1992

HALVA CREAM

Ingredients

1 cup soy cream
2 lemons
2 tbsp oil
2–4 oz halva (depending on sweetness)
crystalized ginger/fruit

Preparation

Liquidize top 4 ingredients and serve in
a glass topped with fruit/ginger.
— *Phoenix Vegetarian B+B, Inch Co Kerry*

Andrew from **Alumni Feedback** organized the tour for **Decadence Within** and
really wanted to come down to Dublin to
play. He got them a gig in Larne, which was a
new place for touring bands to visit.

This was a really slow start to the year after
the almost constant gigs on 1991. Both this gig
and the previous **Slunk** one drew really bad
crowds. **Decadence Within** got £50 for the
Dublin gig. **Alumni Feedback** didn't even get
the comfort of playing to many people and
they travelled home with a lot less money than
they left with.

The **Nessun Dorma** gig the following
month had just as poor a turnout. Both bands
had travelled over in a bus, not the fancy tour bus
and that many bands travel in but a bit like a
school bus (they're the journeys the retired buses
go on in Ireland).

Like Andrew with **Decadence Within**,
Emmet from Cork organized for **Nessun
Dorma** to come over to Ireland and asked us to
accomodate them in Dublin. Charlie's was now

closed to afternoon gigs so we had to try and find
a venue open to allowing "underage people" into
a gig. The Attic wasn't too keen as, even though
the floor had been reinforced, they didn't want
to go through the "hassle" of doing it again.

Peter Quigley had been looking after the
booking of the Grattan and the Fox since **Not
Our World** started playing and he agreed to try
an afternoon gig if it was a Sunday. Saturday is
a traditionally busy shopping day and bars were
uncomfortable compromising local businesses
by allowing loud rock music and encouraging
large congregations outside their establish-
ments while their neighbours tried to get shop-
pers in. This suited **Nessun Dorma** so we tried
for the Grattan.

Sundays in Ireland generally have a lethargic
feel to them. For many it's a lazy day. When very
few people showed up for the gig we were very disappointed. This gig in the Grattan must have
been the hardest gig all three bands have ever
played and no doubt the two touring bands were
very eager to get back into their bus for a rest. The
bus was amazing. It was a renovated old bus that
the band could use for living in if need be.

The atmosphere inside the Grattan was
almost churchlike, very sombre. The crowd
was poor and most people there were not
happy to stay.

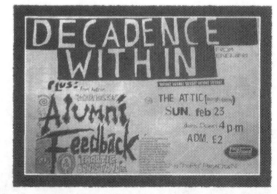

SPERMBIRDS + ONION BREATH + SMH | BARNSTORMERS, MARCH 19, 1992

I was thrilled when **Spermbirds** asked to come over. They had been going for a few years and I suppose I always viewed them as a "big" band, in that they wouldn't need Hope promotions if they wanted to play Ireland.

Robbie Foy was now booking The Attic. He found a new venue called Barnstormers on Capel Street. He bought a PA, put it in there, and was ready to hire it out to bands.

Barnstormers was owned/run by Hell's Angels so some noise and people who looked a little bit "different" was fine by them.

Looking back, Barnstormers was the start of a new era for Hope: Charlie's was gone for the foreseeable future, and The Attic, the Fox and the Grattan were all unsuitable if 100 people were at the gig or if one person wanted to dance. Barnstormers could hold 200 people and it was on the ground floor, a concrete floor. People could dance the night away if they wished.

Spermbirds was a great introductory gig for Robbie and Barnstormers. We took in £425 at the door, the Spermbirds got £240 and everyone seemed happy.

My memories of this are of crowd surfing, a little trouble, and looking over the sea of heads from the back of Barnstormers thinking something is RIGHT here. It was refreshing to see people coming to gigs after the early "disasters" in the year.

STUFFED ONIONS

Ingredients

6 large onions
3 cupfuls breadcrumbs
1/2 cup each fresh sage, parsley, and thyme
1 tbsp paprika
1 cupful mushrooms
1 red bell pepper
olive oil
oil for frying

Preparation

1. Peel the onions and cut the crowns flat.
2. Boil in water for 10 minutes.
3. Chop the fresh herbs and mix in with the breadcrumbs, adding the paprika and around 2–3 tablespoons of olive oil.
4. Finely chop and lightly fry the mushrooms and the pepper, then add them to the breadcrumb mix.
5. Take onions from pot and run them under cold water. Carefully remove the centres of the onions leaving 3–4 layers of a shell remaining. This can be difficult if they've been overboiled and there are certain tricks that can be employed to make it slightly easier than minor surgery, which I'll leave to your imagination and amazing prowess with a small kitchen knife.
6. Chop removed onion finely and add 1/3 of it to your breadcrumb mix. Stuff each onion with as much of the mix as will physically fit, glaze with olive oil place in a pre-greased oven tray. Bake for 30 minutes at 425°F.
7. Eat. Throw dirty plates over wall into neighbors' back garden.

—*Baz, Onion Breath*

SPINY NORMAN QUARTET + SWEET MARY JANE
BARNSTORMERS, MARCH 21, 1992

Two days after getting 140 people to see the **Spermbirds**, 24 turned up to witness two Belfast bands. They were doing an Irish tour and asked to play Dublin. The people in **Spiny Norman Quartet** helped out with Warzone Collective in Belfast and in turn were very active in creating a community up there.

Warzone sprang out of the Belfast Youth + Community Group. That group was started by a gathering of like-minded people with an aspiration to find their own centre. They set about trying to obtain funding and finally got a building. After putting a huge amount of work into it the building played host to a café, venue, rehearsal room and general hive of activity. It has been an inspiration for many. Since then Warzone has had to move to another building, but the group is still very active today.

VEGAN CHEESEY SAUCE

Ingredients

3 tbsp margarine
2~3 tbsp flour
1 tbsp mustard
4 cups soy milk
1 cup yeast flakes

Preparation

1. Melt the marg and stir in the flour and mustard; make sure it's not lumpy.
2. Gradually stir in the milk, stirring constantly so it doesn't go lumpy. Turn the heat up and stir until it thickens.
3. Once it thickens, turn the heat off and add in the yeast flakes.

—*Suzy, Warzone*

EVIL SPINACH POTATO BAKE

Ingredients

3 1/2 lbs frozen spinach
4 1/2 lbs mashed potatoes
2 onions, finely chopped
1/2 bulb of garlic, chopped (or less according to taste)
2 tbsp dried basil
1 cup yeast flakes (optional)
salt and pepper to taste
oil for frying

Preparation

1. Defrost the spinach, cook and mash the potatoes.
2. Fry the onion and garlic in the oil until slightly browned.
3. Put the spinach, herbs and seasoning in with the onions and heat through.
4. Mix thoroughly with the mashed potatoes and yeast flakes.
5. Grease a roasting can and spoon the mixture into it.
6. Smooth the top over with vegan cheese or cheese sauce (see across).
7. Bake in a preheated 350°F oven until browned on top (about 30 minutes).

—*Suzy, Warzone*

JAILCELL RECIPES + DECLINE + UNSOUND
BARNSTORMERS, APRIL 3, 1992

I persuaded Robbie and Barnstormers to host a Saturday afternoon show with no age restrictions. They were hesitant, as they were situated in a commercial street with many shops open for business. Because of the success of **Spermbirds** they agreed to go with an afternoon gig. However the carpet showrooms next door weren't too pleased. The noise was affecting customers' judgement and we had to keep levels down ridiculously low until 5:30—a hard thing to do as the gig started at 3:00.

This was our third time to put a gig on for **Jailcell Recipes** and our third time to lose money on the band. The Belfast Gig Collective were big fans so whenever they asked if **Jailcell** could play we had no option but to say yes.

This gig was Barnstormers first and last Saturday afternoon affair. The owners decided it wasn't worth disturbing the neighbouring businesses. We still couldn't find an affordable venue to put gigs on that wasn't a pub. So, for now, people would have to make do with false IDs. I had gone to school with the "bouncer" in Barnstormers and, thankfully, he turned very few people away.

It wasn't the ideal solution, so with Warzone collective in mind, we decided to start actively looking for our own place. We scoured Dublin for premises suitable to house a vegetarian café that could double up as a venue. We set up a cooperative and applied for as many grants as we could.

VEGAN CHEESEY PASTA

Ingredients

1 lb bag pasta
1 head broccoli, finely chopped
1 lb mushrooms, finely chopped
cheesey sauce
1 cup of yeast flakes
1 tbsp basil
3/4 cup margarine
1/4 cup tahini
1/4 cup water
3 tsp red wine vinegar
3 cloves garlic finely chopped (optional, to taste)
salt and pepper to taste

Preparation

1. Melt margarine in a small saucepan.
2. Slowly stir in the garlic, yeast flakes, basil, vinegar, salt and pepper.
3. Add in a small drop of water to ensure that the sauce maintains a creamy consistency.
4. Let sit on low heat, stirring occasionally.
5. Boil water and cook the pasta.
6. Steam the broccoli in a colander over a pot of boiling water until tender. Alternatively cook in boiling water for 5 minutes.
7. Sauté the mushrooms in hot olive oil and garlic.
8. Drain pasta and place in a large bowl.
9. Add the mushroom and brocolli. Then add the cheese sauce. Either cover and shake or delicately stir well.

—*Ryan Murphy, Gainesville Florida*

WAT TYLER + THATCHER ON ACID | ANARCHY NIGHT CAFÉ, APRIL 23, 1992

OLD UNCLE BEN'S TOFU SCRAMBLE

Ingredients

- 1/2 lb block tofu (wash thoroughly in cold water before use)
- 1 large onion
- 4 cloves garlic
- dark soy sauce
- 1/4 lb mushrooms
- pepper, salt
- Engevita (nutritional yeast flakes)
- olive oil

Preparation

1. Mash up the tofu in a bowl using a fork and add a generous splash of soy sauce. Mix well and set aside.
2. Skin and finely chop the garlic and onion.
3. Pour 1 tbsp olive oil in a non-stick frying pan over a low heat.
4. Add onions and garlic to the pan and cover (using a plate, chopping board, whatever)
5. Chop mushrooms and add to the pan. Keep pan covered. Add a little salt and pepper to the tofu along with a generous heap of Engevita and stir well.
6. Once the contents of the pan are cooking in their own juice, throw in all the other ingredients. Turn up the heat and cook for 5–10 minutes, stirring frequently until golden brown.
7. Serve on toasted farmhouse bread with a glass of orange juice and some strong coffee.

"Recommended listening while preparing: 'For The Roses' LP by Joni Mitchell, and there you have it."
—Ben Thatch

As Sean and Ben had helped out with the *Statement* 12" we decided it would be a good idea if both bands did a tour of Ireland. We got them gigs in Arklow, Belfast, and Dublin. They were travelling over on the Thursday and the people from Anarchy Night Café were willing to let them play.

Wat Tyler had a deserved reputation for being jokers and they were making comments straight away to the crowd. Most didn't care but any **Wat Tyler** gig is a good laugh and one for people not to take too seriously.

Having said that, though, the way they run their band is a perfect statement in itself. Fiercely independent and always willing to help, Sean and **Wat Tyler** became a later influence on Hope.

Wat Tyler

WAT TYLER + THATCHER ON ACID + DOG DAY | BARNSTORMERS, APRIL 26, 1992

"We were playing a gig in Arklow with **Thatcher on Acid** and a band from Wales (whose name escapes me). After the gig in Dublin the previous night, we travelled down during the day. We (**Wat Tyler**) and **Thatch** were sharing the van driven by Protag from **Blyth Power** and his girlfriend Mourmel.

We had nowhere to stay, so at the gig asked if anyone could put us up for the night.

After many requests, no-one came forward so at the end of the gig we had nowhere to stay—there was clearly not room in the van. As we milled around, a local punk told us that he knew a way into the burned out Arklow Lodge Hotel opposite. We had sleeping bags so we decided to stay there. We got in under some corrugated iron at the back and felt around in the dark.

The back wing was derelict but had largely escaped the fire damage. We walked in the dark to the end of the corridor and nearly fell to our deaths one floor below as the central part of the hotel had been gutted by the fire and our corridor just ended in space. We decided to go back to the end two rooms and bed down there. We all bedded down in one room except for Sean who went into a smaller room next door to be by himself (he snores and likes to sleep by himself!).

We talked for a while about how spooky it was, then started to make ghost noises. The conversation went as follows:

Main room: "Whhhoooooooo."
Whhhhooooooo" (Ghost noise!)
Sean: "Shut up, you lot."
Main room: "Whhhoooooooooo. Whhhhooo."
Sean: "Just shut up."
Main room (whispered among ourselves):
"Fucking hell—he is not mucking about, he is really scared."—a bit of giggling.
Main room (loud): "Whhhooo.
Whhhhoooo!"
Sean: "Shut the fuck up!"

Main room (giggling, followed by):
"Whhhoooooooooo. Whhhhhooooooo—"

At that point there was a crashing about and a huge figure appeared in silhouette in the doorway brandishing a club made from a broken table leg. In a faltering voice the apparition said: "Just fucking shut up, okay. Just fucking shut up!"

After a shocked pause, everyone giggled nervously before Ben, from **Thatch**, said:"Sean, what the fuck are you doing? Just look at yourself. You're fucking mental. Just look at yourself." Sean replied: "Its not funny, okay. Just fucking shut up."

Sean went back to his room and after much mirthful discussion and analysis of the events we all went to sleep. When we got up in the morning, Sean was clearly embarrassed and had the hump.

He didn't say anything. We all climbed out of the Hotel at the back onto the steep bank going down to the river. The corners of Sean's mouth pointed towards the floor as he clambered out. As he stepped out he slipped on the wet grass and tumbled to the bottom of the hill, his duvet getting filthy as he slid toward the bottom of the bank amid fits of

Hope Memories Part 1 by Derek Byrne

For me, Hope and **Fugazi** will always be connected—the ideas, the spirit,

the lack of compromise when it comes to doing what they do/did, and the

inspiration that they have been and continue to be. >>

CHAPTER 3

still hope

Fugazi

"I later discovered the fundamentals of Hope—low door prices, all-ages gigs where possible, no guarantees, no bouncers, a whole other way of doing things—not just local bands either; bands came from all over the world to play in pub backrooms, little-used nightclubs and anywhere that would let them play. You didn't know the bands on the poster? Who cared? Support Hope, support the scene, support the bands, take a chance. So many incredible moments, so many great bands, friends that you'd keep for life, so much energy bouncing off the walls, and, of course, Niall and Miriam at the door, chatting away.

I was living in a house in Phibsboro around the time that **NOFX** first came over. Niall was stuck for somewhere for them to stay so we said we'd put them up. In the end I think they went straight on to the next gig, but from then on whenever bands came over with Hope they stayed at our place. If there were a couple of bands then we roped in some friends and neighbours to help out.

The house became one of the band stopovers that you could find all over the world—the band would arrive, we'd feed 'em, they'd play, then they'd hang out at the house. I remember a lot of late night yakking, a lot of really cool, open, intelligent people, and some great music.

At the same time there was *React*—the free sheet started by Niall. Myself and Alan Rosney were doing a fanzine, *Catharsis*, and helping out with a local pirate radio station, Radioactive (which later became DARC). The fanzine came out sporadically, and we wanted to do a monthly free sheet where the record reviews wouldn't be out of date when they saw the light of day, so we copied the *React* idea and *Gearhead Nation* was born; later on Finbar McGloughlin took over from Alan and we put out *GN* monthly for the next few years. *React* stopped somewhere along the way as did *Catharsis*. For me, *GN* was the logical continuation of what had begun with *React*."

—Derek Byrne, *redf* records and Gearhead Nation

Fugazi

CHUMBAWAMBA + FUGAZI + IN MOTION | SFX, MAY 11, 1992

VEG KEBABS

Ingredients

1 lb tofu cut into cubes
about 2 lb veg cut into cubes, e.g., zucchini, small onions, mushrooms, bell peppers, etc.

Marinade:

1 tbsp olive oil
juice & grated rind of 2 limes
2 garlic cloves crushed
1 inch fresh ginger, grated
1 stalk lemongrass, chopped
1 red chili
2 tbsp fresh cilantro

Preparation

1. Mix all marinade ingredients together and pour over tofu—leave to marinate for 2 hours.
2. Cut veg into chunks and add to tofu.
3. Mix and coat with marinade and thread onto skewers.
4. Cook them on a barbecue or under a grill. Leave for five minutes, and add the red bell pepper.
5. If using eggplant rinse it, wash out the salt, chop into bite-size pieces and add to the pan, along with lashings of olive oil. The more oil you add, the softer they seem to get, so it's your call on this.
6. Then add to the skewer.

—*Lou, Chumbawamba*

playing in the 1300 capacity SFX, a venue normally used by big-time promoters MCD, was an achievement. Along with the bands there was a large multimedia extravaganza.

The gig was a benefit for Act-Up and raised over £700. This was a little disappointing. More funds could have been raised BUT this money was pumped into information instead. The ticket for the gig acted as a full color multi-page information leaflet about AIDS awareness (something not seen at many gigs) including how to use hypodermic needles. It cost a lot of money to print and it caused a lot of controversy.

The Jesuit owners of the SFX wanted the ticket withdrawn. They said that some of the information on it was too explicit for them. We agreed to print a second ticket, which we showed to the Jesuits—but the original tickets stayed in circulation and the Jesuits reluctantly agreed not to pull the plug. They gave their final decision one week before the gig.

The conspiracy theorists among us leaped to attention when the owners mentioned in conversation that the main hirer of the building had been in touch with them about the gig. It certainly brought a smile to our faces. This gig was the culmination of more than two months of planning involving a lot of people, including the Ents Officer of Trinity College. There were over 1300 people present at a cost of £4.50 a head. This was half the usual price for a gig in the venue.

As I looked down into the audience during **Fugazi**'s set, I felt we really could do anything we wanted to—as long as we did it together.

This gig was a highlight, I must admit. To save **Fugazi** from America, **Chumbawamba** from England and **In Motion** from Dublin all

(This gig has been written about in many places, including the liner notes of a Chumbawamba CD, a book about the music scene of Washington DC, and the pages of Irish political satire magazine *Phoenix*. —*Ed.*)

NOFX + GAS FARM + ARNHEIM | BARNSTORMERS, MAY 31, 1992

Less than 3 weeks after the SFX it was back to basics for the 2nd visit of NOFX to Ireland. Pat spent an age with NOFX outside Barnstormers afterwards . . . talking about food. They then went off to some party and were missing for a while the following morning.

SPINACH AND CAULIFLOWER BHAJI

Ingredients

1 cauliflower
1 lb fresh spinach (forget frozen or canned, it's an insult to any spinach fiend)
4 tbsp olive oil
2 large onions
2 garlic cloves
1 inch ginger
1 tbsp cayenne pepper (at least!!! You know how some people are with hot food—although if you're a sadist like myself, then pile it on!!!)
1 tbsp each cumin and turmeric
2 tbsp coriander
1 can chopped tomatoes
1 1/3 cups vegetable stock
salt and freshly ground black pepper

Preparation

1. Divide cauliflower into small florets, discarding hard central stalk. Trim the stalks from the spinach leaves.
2. Heat the oil in a large pot. Add the onions and cauliflower and fry gently for 3-5 minutes, stiring frequently.
3. Add the ginger, garlic and spices and cook for a further 2 minutes. Stir in the stock, tomatoes and salt and pepper.
4. Bring to the boil, then cover, reduce heat and simmer for 8 minutes.
5. Add spinach to the pan, stirring to wilt the leaves. Cover again and simmer for 8–10 minutes, until cauliflower is tender. Serve hot.

"This classic Indian side dish was unashamedly lifted straight from an Indian vegetarian cook book because of its simplicity, and the all important fact that it doesn't take very long. The original claims that this serves four. Take that as meaning it really serves two . . . Who are all these people with tiny stomachs????"

—*BOZ, Steam Pig + Onion Breath*

INSTIGATORS + THE BIKE THIEVES + BRINSKILL BOMBEAT | THE ROXEY, JUNE 26, 1992

TAHINI STIR-FRY

Tofu

Take one block of extra-firm tofu, drain out the water, and place on a cutting board or flat surface on top of a paper towel. Incline the cutting board slightly so that water will run off. Put a paper towel and another flat surface on top of the tofu and a weight on top of that (about 5 lbs: a phone book is good). Leave to drain. With less water, the tofu will fry better and is more likely not to come apart while cooking.

Rice

Short-grained brown rice is my favorite by far. Brown rice has more taste, more fiber, and more protein than white rice. Short grain has more tendency to stay in separate nuggets once cooked. Rinse the rice in a strainer before cooking. Use two cups water for each cup of rice. Get the water boiling. Add rice and stir. Turn the heat down to a very low setting (on a gas stove, just above the lowest you can go without being afraid the flame will go out). Cover with a tight lid, and leave for 45 minutes. However you cook it, get it started before you do the rest of the meal! You want 2 (or 3 if you love rice) cups of rice (the dry measurement) for this meal.

Sauce

1/2 cup tahini, 1/2 cup soy sauce
2 tbsp sugar, 2 tbsp sesame oil
1 1/2 tbsp red wine vinegar
1 tbsp fresh ginger, chopped
1 tbsp fresh garlic, chopped
Combine all above ingredients in a jar with a lid, and shake vigorously for a minute or two. If your tahini is very thick, the sauce may need a little water added to run freely.

Stir-Fry Ingredients

tofu—1 block cut into strips (about 2 inches by 1/2 inch) or cubes
3 cups broccoli, chopped
3 cups purple cabbage, chopped
2 cups carrots, chopped
2 cups mushrooms, chopped
2 cups onion, chopped (or 1 cup chopped scallion)
2 tbsp sesame seeds
1 tsp ginger, chopped
2 tsp garlic, chopped

Preparation

1. Toast sesame seeds, stirring or shaking constantly, in a dry pan on high heat, until they start to pop. Set aside.
2. Add ginger, garlic, and tofu to a pan with a good amount of oil (peanut oil is best). Fry on medium-high heat for about 7–10 minutes, or until the tofu browns slightly.
3. Add carrots and onions. Fry another 7–10 minutes.
4. Add remaining ingredients, and fry until vegetables seem cooked but retain some crispness. Stir very often.
5. Add in the pre-made sauce (across page)—vary amount depending on your taste, and finish stir-frying. (If you have remaining sauce it will be good later on rice or anything else, straight out of the fridge, or your guests can add more individually to their servings.)
6. Turn off heat. Stir in toasted sesame seeds. Feeds 3–5.

—Arik Grier, Fat Day

Deko got a new venue going called The Roxey, off Capel Street in the Smithfield markets area of Dublin. He put on gigs there every Friday. **The Instigators** were looking to come over to play on a Friday so I asked Deko if they could play there. He readily agreed.

The band were nearly as interested in watching Denmark's surprise victory in the European Soccer Championships as they were in playing tonight's gig.

The Bike Thieves from Germany also played on the bill. They were on holiday in Ireland at the time and, as they were in town, asked if they could play. No-one objected, even though we had no idea what they would sound like. They were okay and got £6 for their troubles.

Paranoid Visions and their subsequent bands, like **Striknien DC**, found it very hard to get gigs at times, so Deko got around this by finding his own places. He would become friendly with a bar manager and would get one night or so to put on gigs. Sometimes the venue doubled up as rehearsal spaces (or even recording rooms) for bands.

Deko was a central figure in punk rock in Dublin. He was always outspoken and Hope was one of the things he sometimes complained about, but in all honesty he was always helpful whenever I asked him anything.

Even though the Roxey was there every Friday we continued to hire Barnstormers. It was cheaper (Roxey cost £100 to hire) and was more accessible for many people. It was also available on different nights. The Roxey was seen as a punk venue and Hope began to be seen as some sort of "student thing." It was something we never shook off and was a breeding ground for future wars of words.

Ian MacKaye, Fugazi

MR. T. EXPERIENCE + DOG DAY + HEADCLEANER + CROSSBREED
BARNSTORMERS, JULY 4, 1992 + JULY 19, 1992

It's funny how things go through waves but the latter half of each year always seemed to have had more bands looking to travel to Ireland.

Both of these gigs had decent crowds. **Mr. T. Experience** were in the mold of **Green Day**, who were starting to get a lot of popular attention (put it down to that gig in The Attic!!) and much like the hype of Seattle and Dublin (in the **U2** era) there was talk of all bands from San Francisco being signed up by majors.

At this stage there seemed to be more Dublin bands than ever looking for gigs in their hometown. They were bands with a wide variety of musical styles too, which was nice.

At the **Fugazi** gig in the SFX a person introduced himself as Murt Flynn from New Ross. He was interested in putting some gigs on here. We subsequently met up to talk about the possibilities.

Headcleaner were the first band to travel to New Ross and it was the start of many great gigs in Gallivan's.

Headcleaner were willing to travel anywhere and were unbelievably keen. This was the first of their two paid-for trips to Ireland and they got to see quite a bit of the country.

CUBAN MOJITO

Ingredients

large measure of Havana Club rum*
handful of fresh mint leaves
1 tbsp sugar
ice
soda water

Preparation

1. Put mint, sugar and rum into large glass.
2. Mash together.
3. Fill glass with ice.
4. Top up with soda water.
5. Drink.
6. Go to 1.

*Not Bacardi unless you are Yankee capitalist scum.

—*Hugh McCabe, Crossbreed*

MDC + CIUNAS | BARNSTORMERS, AUG. 1, 1992

MDC, wow! In Barnstormers on Capel Street! This was a wild gig. "Corporate Deathburger," "John Wayne was a Nazi"—being played live in Dublin! The venue was packed. The gig was great fun. There was plenty of dancing and even a small melee couldn't dampen the atmosphere.

When Christy asked us about doing **MDC** I was very excited. I had been a fan for a long time.

Mick McCaughen felt the same way. Mick the Mohawk (as he was known for quite a while) is a journalist who travels mainly in Central and South America commentating on the political situation there. He was a huge **MDC** fan. He was in Ireland at the time and the band stayed with him.

As for the gig, it was one where I got to see little of the band in question. I was collecting the door money at the back of the venue. The whole crowd were between me and the band. If I wanted to see any of the band's set I had to push, shove and weave my way through a myriad of people. When I got to my vantage point I would need to be somewhere else to sort something out. Generally for gigs like this I stood at the back of the hall and watched on.

With **MDC** it was like that and I watched on as Barnstormers erupted to the music.

LENTIL SOUP (VEGGIE ITALIAN STYLE)

Ingredients

2 cups dried lentils
3 cloves garlic, minced
1 small onion minced
16 oz can crushed plum tomatoes
1 cup brown rice or 1 cup elbow macaroni
1/4 cup virgin olive oil
1 large bay leaf
salt, pepper, and hot pepper

Preparation

1. Place olive oil in 3 qt pot. Add onion stirring occasionally until golden. Add garlic. Do not allow to brown.
2. Add can of tomatoes and lentils and bay leaf and 1 quart of water and seasonings.
3. Cook until lentils are tender (about 1 1/2 hours), stirring often. Add more water if needed.
3. Boil rice (or macaroni) separately in salted water. When cooked drain off water and add to lentil soup.
4. Feel free to dice and add other veggies. Try eggplant, carrots or celery.

—Dave Dictor, MDC

HEAVENLY + THE PECADILLOES | BARNSTORMERS, AUG. 15, 1992

FRUIT CAKES

Ingredients

4 cups mixed golden raisins, currants, and raisins
1 3/4 cups water
2/3 cup oil
2 3/4 cups self-rising flour
1/2 cup chopped almonds
1 tbsp molasses
grated rind of 1 lemon
2 tsp ground mixed spice
1/3 cup brown sugar
3 tbsp sherry

Preparation

1. Grease and line 6-inch round cake pan.
2. Place all ingredients, except sherry, in a basin and beat well until evenly mixed.
3. Pour into pan and bake for about 2 hours 300°F, until risen and firm to touch.
4. Allow to cool slightly in the pan then spoon the sherry over the cake and leave in pan until completely cold.

"Unlike a traditional fruit cake, this cake does not keep for very long."

—Amelia Fletcher, Heavenly

Two weeks after the political hardcore noise of **MDC** came **Heavenly**. Rising from the ashes of **Talulah Gosh**, **Heavenly** were pure unashamed pop. There was something infectious about both them and **Talulah Gosh**.

This provided a great opportunity to put forward music of different styles. It was a chance to counteract a criticism being put forward about Hope that we only went for one type of music. In truth, we were still only going for bands that requested us to help them get a gig in Ireland. Other than that there was no taste test.

I was really happy putting a flier for the four August 1992 gigs into *React*. There was a huge diversity in bands, their sound and their lyrics. However, there was a common bond between **MDC**, **Heavenly**, **Dawson**, **Long Fin Killie**, **Herb Garden** and **Decadence Within** (all the bands to travel in August): independence. People didn't need to sign to some huge record label to get gigs outside their own city/country. People like Hope were more than willing to help them with it.

Leagues was regularly helping out now and he brought his friend Johnny from **Powerful Mellow** to see these "new" bands. Johnny recorded many Barnstormers gigs on his 4-track recorder. The **Heavenly** recording is perfect.

As an aside, I think **Heavenly** were the first band we put on that used keyboards.

DECADENCE WITHIN + HERB GARDEN + THE COLLECTORS
BARNSTORMERS, AUG. 23, 1992

Decadence Within and **Herb Garden** both returned to our shores. This time they played together as their dates clashed.

Paying money out at the end of a gig was always pretty difficult, especially when there were very few people at the gig. Both bands had traveled over from England and received £45 for their troubles. Thankfully they had gigs in New Ross, Belfast, Larne and Cork to help boost their funds but getting £45 in the capital city was a bit embarrassing for all concerned.

We always ensured that bands got some food. This usually entailed making some sandwiches and whoever was putting the band up would cook them something later.

Derek was always offering to help with gigs and he lived near town. He allowed many bands to stay at his house and was always accommodating towards them. He and his housemates made the stay of many bands more comfortable; for that they should be thanked. They became the first people other than the bands not to pay in. It was our only way of saying thanks: £2–3 off getting into a gig!!!!!

APPLE PECAN COFFEE CAKE

Ingredients

3 cups whole wheat pastry flour
1 cup fructose
1 tbsp cinnamon
3/4 tsp nutmeg
1/2 tsp allspice
3/4 cup margarine
1 1/4 cup soy milk
3 tsp baking powder
1 apple, peeled and sliced into thin wedges
1/2 cup chopped pecans

Preparation

1. Preheat oven to 375°F and grease a 9 x 9" glass baking dish.
2. Mix flour, fructose, cinnamon, nutmeg, allspice, and margarine in a bowl until mixture resembles crumbs. Remove 1 cup of this to use later as topping.
3. Add baking powder to the bowl and mix well. Then add soy milk and mix well.
4. Pour batter into pan, and layer with apple slices.
5. Sprinkle reserved topping over the apples, then sprinkle with pecans.
6. Bake for 40 minutes or until toothpick inserted in centre comes out clean. Oven times vary considerably so check it at 30 minutes and every 5 minutes thereafter.

—Niall, Hope Promotions

ALICE DONUT + GOUT + BRAWL | BARNSTORMERS, AUG. 30, 1992

THREE BEAN CURRY

Ingredients

3 cups raw beans—flagelot, kidney and lima (You can use canned beans but they are more expensive)
1 onion, chopped
clove garlic
some oil for frying
2 tbsp curry powder
1 can tomatoes
2 1/2 cups rice
parsley

Preparation

1. Most beans benefit from an initial soaking before cooking. It speeds up the cooking time and makes them more digestible. Put the beans in a large bowl, fill with water and leave overnight. The following day rinse the beans with cold water in a colander. Cover with water and cook them in a large pot for an hour.
2. Cook the rice seperately. Add rice to 8 cups of boiling water. Bring back to the boil and simmer for about 20 mins. Drain water off.
3. Fry the onion in hot oil with the garlic.
4. Add curry powder and cook for a moment.
5. Throw in tomatoes.
6. Now add the cooked beans. Serve when it is heated thoroughly.

"Note: You could sprinkle chopped parsley over each serving as it looks nice and is full of iron."
— Clodagh, Hope Collective

And so it continued. Bands that had a good name attracted the crowds; unheard-of bands drew much smaller numbers. Few people were willing to take the risk, especially if the band were not American.

Alice Donut was both heard of and American so they were bound to get a good crowd, which they did. They spent a couple of days in Ireland and got to play Cork. This was great, as many American bands only came to play Dublin and Belfast. They enjoyed themselves so much in Derek's house that they didn't want to leave Irealnd.

Gout asked to come up from Kilkenny to play sometime and this seemed like a good opportunity for them to make the journey. **Gout** was to become quite popular and indeed came up to live in Dublin. For this gig, though, they got a lift up from a parent after school and went straight home after.

Murt's band **Brawl** was the other band on the night. **Brawl** were really active in their area, putting on gigs and eventually releasing their own album so it was great to give them the opportunity to play to a decent crowd in Dublin.

There seems to be a better mentality from people in bands outside Dublin. **Brawl** were typical of this. They didn't wait for others to do things for them: they just got out and did it themselves.

DAWSON + LONG FIN KILLIE
THE ATTIC, AUG. 13 1992 | BARNSTORMERS, SEPT. 11, 1993

When my parents bought me my trusty typewriter in 1990 the first band I wrote to was **Dawson**. I corresponded regularly over the years with Jer of the band. I loved their wild discordant noise. I took some copies of their records to sell and kept talking about them to anyone that would listen.

When Jer asked if I could help organize something for them and fellow Glaswegians **Long Fin Killie** I was over the moon. When he asked for it to be on August 13 I was devastated.

Miriam and I were due to be in Mayo that day in the middle of a holiday with her family.

We had a long discussion about it and agreed to get the train home that day. Thankfully we got back in time to see **Dawson** in Dublin. What a privilege.

Not too many others got to witness that privilege but it was their loss, undoubtedly. Amazing!

Barnstormers the following year was equally thrilling.

ARTICHOKE CASSEROLE WITH PINE NUTS

Ingredients

- 3 tsp olive oil
- 4 vegetarian bacon slices, cut into strips (optional)
- 1 large onion
- 3 cloves garlic
- 1 lb ripe plum tomatoes, skinned and chopped (see tip)
- 2 cups vegetable stock
- 4 x 14 oz artichoke hearts, drained and halved
- sea salt and black pepper to taste
- 1 oz pine nuts, toasted

Preparation

1. In a small frying pan heat 1 tsp of the oil and cook bacon over a medium heat until lightly browned. Remove from pan and set to one side.
2. Heat the remaining oil in a large saucepan and soften the onion and garlic over a low heat for 5–7 minutes.

Sir in the prepared tomatoes and cook uncovered for 10 minutes or until the tomatoes are reduced to a sauce consistency.

3. Add the stock and season with salt and pepper. Bring to the boil, add artichokes, cover and simmer for 12–15 minutes.
4. Turn casserole out into a serving dish and sprinkle with the cooked bacon pieces and pine nuts. Serve immediately.

Skinning Tomatoes:

Put tomatoes into a large bowl and cover with boiling water. Leave to stand for thirty seconds. Lift out one by one and pierce the skin with a sharp knife; the skin will peel off easily.

—*Luke Sutherland,*
Long Fin Killie + Mogwai

CRANE + MEXICAN PETS | BARNSTORMERS, SEPT. 20, 1992

SPICY PLUM, PEAR AND GINGER CRUMBLE

Ingredients

6 plums
2 pears
1 apple
1/4 cup apple juice concentrate
2 tsp finely grated fresh ginger
2 tsp cinnamon
1 tsp nutmeg
1 pinch ground black pepper
1/4 cup water
1/2 cup oats
1/4 cup whole wheat flour
1/4 cup vegan marg
1/4 cup fair trade Demarera sugar
1 tsp cinnamon
fistful juicy raisins
fistful sunflower seeds

Preparation

1. Mix first 8 ingredients together and simmer for 10–15 minutes.
2. Rub together oats, marg, sugar, flour and cinnamon, then add raisins and seeds to the mix.
3. Pour fruit into ovenproof dish and evenly distribute crumble mix on top. Cook for 35 mins approx at 350°F.

Serve with loads of vanilla soy dessert.

—*Steve, Crane, with a little help from Rosa*

Crane were good friends with **Slum Turkeys** and after that band's successful tour the previous year they looked to come over and do something similar. **Mexican Pets** had also become friendly with **Slum Turkeys** during this period, after travelling to play Manchester at singer Paul Morley's invitation.

So when **Crane** came over to play some gigs it seemed opportune for **Mexican Pets** to accompany them. They became bosom buddies for five days as they play the Anarchy Night Café, Cork, New Ross, Belfast and Barnstormers.

Crane did one extra daytime gig. This was a bizarre afternoon performance in Our Price records. A friend, Pete Murphy, worked there and he liked **Crane**. I asked if there was a possibility of the band playing there and, lo and behold, the management agreed. The band got £50 and won over a few people.

After the tour **Mexican Pets** and **Crane** were like patients leaving hospital. They had become dependant on each other and had grown rather fond of the company. Plenty of promises to stay in touch were made, promises I'm not sure were ever carried through, but both bands will keep good memories of this Irish tour with them.

JAWBREAKER + THE COLLECTORS + ACE | BARNSTORMERS, SEPT. 26, 1992

Jawbreaker were the third band on Lookout records to visit in less than a year. They were another band who subsequently went on to sign to a major record label.

The Collectors, from Belfast, had played a couple of months previously with **Decadence Within**. As there was such a poor crowd at that gig it seemed only right to get them back down again to give them the opportunity of letting more than 30 people hear what they sounded like. They even managed to get £20 for their efforts. This was £20 more than they were given the previous time they travelled to Dublin to play.

GUACAMOLE

Ingredients

2 soft avocados
1/4 freshly squeezed lemon juice (1 tbsp)
1/2 jalapeño pepper
1/2 red onion, finely chopped
1 tomato, finely chopped
fresh cilantro, very finely chopped
olive oil and salt to taste

Preparation

1. Mash avocados in a bowl with a fork.
2. Add lemon juice.
3. Mince the jalapeño pepper and mix in (de-seed it if you don't want it too hot).
4. Add the red onion and tomato.
5. Finally, most crucial, sprinkle cilantro liberally.
6. You can add a dash of olive oil and salt to taste.

—Blake, Jawbreaker + Jets To Brazil

DONKEY + REVENGE OF THE CARROTS | BARNSTORMERS, OCT.9, 1992

DREAMY DONKEY DAL

Ingredients

2 cups red lentils
1 onion, chopped
3 cloves garlic, chopped
1 small piece ginger, chopped
1 can peeled and chopped tomatoes
1/2 tsp turmeric
1/2 tsp chili powder (or add/subtract to
   personal taste)
salt (add at own pleasure for personal
taste)
oil for frying
water

Preparation

1. Boil the lentils in a pan with sufficient water to just cover the lentils.
2. Whilst this is happening, fry the
   onions, garlic and ginger.
3. When the lentils have started to boil,
   add the tomatoes and stir.
4. When the lentils have achieved a soft
   texture, add the onion/garlic/ginger
   mix. Stir.
5. Add a bit of turmeric. Add salt and
   chilli powder to own taste/satisfac-
   tion. Drain any excess water before
   serving.

—*Ajay Sagaar, Donkey*

The first time I met Ajay he was throwing pieces of paper up in the air in perfect time to **Membranes** songs, no mean feat I can tell you. He travelled everywhere with the **Membranes**, going to as many of their gigs as possible, until they were looking for a bass player and needed to search no further than their audience.

After leaving the **Membranes** he left his hometown of Manchester for Amsterdam, where he swapped Manchester United for Ajax and joined **Donkey**. He wanted **Donkey** to come to Ireland with **Revenge of the Carrots** and we arranged it.

This gig was another one of those moments when I questioned the purpose of Hope. Here were two excellent bands trying to do something a little bit different while remaining interesting, and being ignored by Dublin audiences.

I felt so bad for the people in both bands. They didn't care, but after traveling from Holland I felt it would have been nice to play to more than 30 people. Although I always said not to expect anything from people, deep down I wanted everyone to like **Donkey**.

This was the 26th Dublin gig of 1992 that Hope had put on. The 26th time that year that we had asked people to pay into a gig and people were being choosy. They obviously felt that their £3 could be better spent elsewhere.

DOWNCAST + GROUNDSWELL | BARNSTORMERS, NOV. 4, 1992

After 16 gigs in eight-and-a-half months in Barnstormers this was a depressing one to finish the year on. As you will read on the next page, **Downcast** were not on friendly terms with each other and that carried forward onto the stage and also in any activities we had with the band. It was a nightmare from an organisational point of view.

I only learned that the band were having difficulties when I was assembling this book and for years I had held an opinion on the band based on their personal feelings at the end of a long tour. Funny how wrongly one can judge others after a couple of hours.

People still talk about the **Downcast** gig and how the singer left the stage crying. They think that it was "emo" or something. The music was all about feelings and he gave it everything. I would have preferred a chat but that wasn't to be tonight.

Still, no matter what was going on with the band on the night, the fact that we had put on an average of two gigs a month all featuring bands from outside the country and who otherwise may not have had the chance to visit Ireland was pleasing. Barnstormers was ideal for these touring bands.

VEGETABLE CURRY

Ingredients

garlic, finely chopped
1 onion
salt and pepper to taste
1/4 cup margarine
1-2 tbsp curry powder (to suit taste)
1 can coconut milk
a few yams/sweet potatoes
oil
any veg

Preparation

1. Sautée garlic and onion in oil.
2. Add salt and pepper, cook for 2 minutes.
3. Add margarine and curry powder. Cook for 1 more minute.
4. Add coconut milk, stir and cover. Let this cook for as long as you can stand it. The best I ever made cooked over night. You can let it sit in the fridge for a day if you want to.
5. Whenever you're about an hour away from dinner, put a couple of yams or sweet potatoes in the oven. Roast until tender.
6. Take them out and carefully cut away the top and remove some of the flesh. a spoon works well to scoop it out. If you are encountering difficulties, you haven't baked it long enough—it should scoop right out.
7. Take enough to leave a good hole in the yam but don't go down to the skin on the other side. Add all of this scooped stuff to the curry and mix it in. Take it out of the pan and scoop it back into the yam. Pop a couple of green onions in the top or some carrot slices or whatever. Make them spike out of the top.
8. Bake again for about 15 minutes or so (until the top starts to get golden brown).

"Note: you can add anything to the mix and whatever won't fit back in the yams can be eaten later for breakfast."   Kevin, Downcast

THE REAL TRUTH BEHIND THE GIG
DOWNCAST/GROUNDSWELL, MARIANNE HOFSTETTER

"I had joined **Downcast** in the UK, on the last leg of their European tour, sometime in the early nineties. I don't even remember the year. It was miserable and cold and the band was doing very badly. On day one of the tour, Brent, the guitarist, had decided that he didn't want to be on tour. He wanted to be home with his girlfriend.

So, in order to let everyone know that he was here against his will, he stood on stage stone-faced, played his riffs, showing no emotions at all. Nobody in the van talked to him. I don't think I said a single word to him in ten days.

It was beyond awkward. It didn't help that most of the shows in the UK had been cancelled. Everybody was feeling dismal. Then, in Belfast, I got very, very sick. So sick, in fact, that one night while staying in somebody's house I was sure I wasn't gonna make it through. I had such a high fever I honestly thought I was going to die.

Needless to say, I made it and we arrived in Dublin. I went inside the club and had a look around, but it was still hours till the show, so I decided to take a nap in the van. At this point I'd like to say that it's really unwise to tour with cargo pants, because those stupid pockets on the side of your leg really hurt when you're trying to sleep across 3 seats. Anyways, not surprisingly, I slept right through the show.

I was awoken by Kevin (the singer) ripping the door open and throwing himself on the floor in the back of the van. He was bawling. I never really talked to him about it, but I think he had simply reached the end of the line.

He couldn't take it anymore. Kent, who had also been on tour with them, later told me that there had almost been a fist fight between Brent and Kevin. And apparently Kevin just ran outside during the show. What an undignified end to such a great band. Because that was it. It was over. And I had slept through it.

We had the next day off and stayed in a very nice house with a bunch of awesome people. All the time I had been aching to take a shower or a bath and now, finally, we were at a place that was nice and warm.

Except that, by then, I was feeling so weak I was unable to even make it upstairs to the bathroom. So, while everyone spent the day sight-seeing, I sat on the settee alone, crying quietly and feeling sorry for myself. When I got back and went to see a doctor, the first thing he did was check my armpits for track marks. I must have looked so fucked-up he thought I was a junkie. It turned out I had pneumonia. Fun!

And that's what I remember about Dublin. I swore that one day I would go back and really see the place. And I know, some day I will."

— *Marianne Hofstetter*

GROUNDSWELL + DOG DAY + PECADILLOES + WORMHOLE
SURF WEASEL + UNEASE + SHANKS + TREEHOUSE
THE FLEET, OCT. 29, NOV. 5, NOV. 12, DEC. 13, 1992

A city center bar, The Fleet, was starting to put on gigs so Leagues booked four nights there. Up to now Hope hadn't concentrated on putting on Dublin bands unless it was for a benefit but these Fleet gigs were a departure from that.

It was a nice little venue but it didn't last into the new year. Each floor had a different function room and the owners didn't appreciate the noise levels from live music.

English band **Surf Weasel** looked to come over and played there. The Fleet and sister venues like The Attic, The Grattan and The Fox were ideal for bands starting off. For £30-£40 you got a room with PA The only failing was that they were all bars with the sole purpose of the owner being to sell alcohol. The Fleet (now called Doyle's) has periodically opened its doors for live music since but usually changes its mind after a short while.

Surf Weasel also played Mulligans Bar, which had just opened its doors to gigs. This was the latest venue that Deko had found. Its location wasn't great, in that it was out of the way in a run-down area of Dublin. Ideally that shouldn't matter for a venue, but unfortunately, for many people it did.

Mulligans also doubled up as a rehearsal room and studio, which Deko co-ordinated. Many bands recorded there and released tapes on Deko's label FOAD.

Nineteen-ninety-two ended with Hope having hosted 33 paying gigs in Dublin. We helped co-ordinate Irish tours for bands with the involvement of people in New Ross, Cork, Larne, Belfast, Derry, Arklow, Trinity College, Bolton Street College, and Our Price Records. Oh, and a record was released as well.

DUNCES APPLE CRUMBLE

Ingredients:

- 1 1/2 cups plain flour
- 3/4 cup brown sugar/caster sugar
- 1 cup soy margarine, cubed
- pinch salt
- 1 lb/6 or 7 apples peeled, with core removed
- 4 tbsp brown sugar/caster sugar
- 1/2 tsp ground cinnamon

Preparation

1. Preheat oven to 350°F.
2. Mix flour, sugar, and salt in a bowl.
3. Rub in margarine till mix resembles fine bread crumbs.
4. Cut apples into segments.
5. Mix in a separate bowl with brown sugar and cinnamon, until segments are coated.
6. Spread evenly in a 7" or 9" baking pan or whatever baking dish you've got handy.
7. Spread crumble over the top, don't press it down.
8. Bake in the oven for 40 minutes to an hour, until crumble is browned (not burnt!) and apples are bubbling underneath.
9. Serve warm with vegan ice cream.

"I don't have any vegan recipes, but my friend Wendy is a master cook. I can personally testify that her Dunces Apple Crumble rules."

—Leagues

NOT FOR MATERIAL GAIN

"It was largely, perhaps ultimately, about communication. Fanzines, non-profit gigs, independent vinyl releases, demo tapes, information on vegetarianism, veganism, environmental issues and anti-fascist organizations: looking back, Hope's most prevalent currency was ideas.

And despite habitual bouts of bitchiness, Hope was designed and maintained as an ego-free entity. I mean, it was never just about pushing what it had produced or organized, it was also a catalyst for the do-it-yourself ideal. It was a living, breathing, practitioner of these sentiments, one that impressed the idea of a self-sufficient network that could exist beyond the increasingly one-dimensional and elitist nature of the corporate mainstream.

As a teenager in the early '90s harbouring a swelling love affair with music, my first encounter with Hope was via its pamphlet newsletter *React*. I soon discovered that the existence of *React* meant a trip to Freebird Records on Eden Quay wasn't wasted, even if I had no money to spend on records (as was often the case). *React* was free, always free and "Not For Material Gain," an interesting and unusual concept even way back in pre-Celtic Tiger Ireland.

Incited by the jumbled collection of opinions, reviews and information cut-and-pasted and photocopied on a folded-over A4 sheet of paper, I took pen to paper, in a bold retort to my instinctive apathy. The result was a (most likely) scrawled, incoherent yet enthused missive of questions, ideas and congratulations posted to *React*.

Offer angst a little direction and it can take you marvellous places. I soon discovered that Niall's reply didn't disappoint. Nor did the series of exchanged letters that followed. His envelopes were usually home made, recycled junk mail emblazoned with hilariously tacky consumer slogans (this, I thought, was a cute encapsulation of the idea of reclaiming the waste of a spurious commercial society and utilising it for positive means). And they were stuffed with flyers advertising gigs for bizarrely named bands I had never heard of before (**Thatcher On Acid**, **Frogs of War**, **Gorilla Biscuits**, **Spiny Norman Quartet**).

But rather than just settle for waiting for my copy of *React* to arrive in the post every couple of weeks, I embraced the D.I.Y. code and produced *Fudge*, my own 'zine. Although it only lasted one issue, I think it was a bountiful issue. And my desire to write about music was firmly established. I began to attend more Hope events, sometimes helping with posters and flyers, eventually going on to organise my own series of Hope gigs in the Fleet Bar in Dublin, where a lovely man by the name of Peter Quigley booked the venue. It was mostly Irish acts, many of whom had difficulty getting gigs anywhere else, but who went on to form and play in many of the most exciting bands in the country today (**Joan of Arse**, **The Last Post**, **The Redneck Manifesto**, **Large Mound**, **Decal**).

There were numerous highlights from those days: seeing **Alice Donut** blow the roof off Barnstormers, the unbelievably messy censorship politics of the **Fugazi** Act-Up benefit in the SFX (it all worked out fine in the end), the release of the **Statement** EP, **Heavenly** in Barnstormers (providing a little lite relief for us pop-kids!). A very rewarding time, it offered me not only an education in music, a social forum, life-long friendships and an excuse to hang out in town, it also presented me a sense of responsibility, for which I will be eternally grateful.

Ten years later I have a shoebox full of memories and, more pertinently, some of the better lessons learned in life."

—Leagues O'Toole, May 2002

HEADCLEANER + HOLEMASTERS + SLUNK + FLEXIHEAD
BARNSTORMERS, FEB. 24, 1993 + MAY 24, 1993

Headcleaner used many of the contacts they had made to organize an Irish tour. I loved their enthusiasm. They were willing to travel anywhere for a gig. They became regular visitors to the country and struck up many friendships. They may not be a big-name band or hugely popular but they were able to visit many parts of Europe on free holidays and have a great time doing so.

Not as many bands looked to come over this year. We were happy with that as my health was starting to improve and Miriam, Pat, Joe and I were trying to find a premises. We had an idea that it would be good to have our own place for gigs and tried to figure out the best way of making it happen. Finance came into the equation so we decided to start a co-op and look at ways of getting funding. We expanded the idea into a café and saw that you could readily obtain grants to run a business. Everything was flowing except the main ingredient: a suitable premises. Because we were getting funding everything had to be above board. Therefore any prospective place had to meet all the necessary health regulations (or have the ability to meet them).

We spent a lot of time putting together business plans, setting up a cooperative and putting together the relevant paperwork for grants. Many afternoons were spent over coffee discussing the price of potatoes.

CHILI BEANS

Ingredients

2 tbsp olive oil
1 large onion, chopped
1 garlic clove, crushed
1 tbsp hot chili powder
1 tbsp all-purpose flour
1 tbsp tomato paste
14 oz can chopped tomatoes, or fresh tomatoes (better)
14 oz can kidney beans, drained
1/2 cup vegetable stock
chopped fresh parsley

Preparation

1. Heat the oil in the frying pan and cook the onion and garlic for about 2 minutes.
2. Stir in the chili powder and flour into the onion and garlic, and cook for a further 2 minutes, stirring constantly.
3. Stir in the tomato paste and chopped tomatoes, rinse the kidney beans and drain.
4. Then add to the pan with the hot vegetable stock.
5. Cover and cook for the final 12 minutes, stirring from time to time.
6. Garnish with chopped parsley.
7. Serve with rice or pasta.

—*Dave Kennedy, Holemasters + Crossbreed*

CORNERSHOP + WHEEL + JAM JAR JAIL
FIBBER MAGEES, FEB. 28, 1993

Technically this isn't a Hope gig but we arranged the accommodation and made the provision for **Cornershop** to play in the Anarchy Night Café. The band was looking to play Dublin on that date, which was a Thursday. Rather than clashing with Anarchy Night Café, which was getting regularly good crowds, we asked could they be put on the bill. This was readily agreed.

The people behind the Anarchy Night Café had a similar motto to Hope: "We are not promoters, we are people—just like you." They went to a lot of our gigs so we knew they'd be keen on helping.

Cornershop had been getting plenty of attention from the British music press, which was interesting from our point of view. We weren't too used to dealing with bands that garnered such interest. All we knew about Cornershop was that they had a link to the **Membranes**. Our base line, though, was they weren't on a major record label (at the time) so we were happy to help.

The major label thing left us open time and again for criticism. It grew and grew as people were questioning our activities. For me, I felt I just didn't want to deal with big record labels. Hope never signed a "contract" and never gave cast-iron guarantees. Sometimes we would have a good idea of how many people would go to the gig and would pass that info on to the band. It was a nice level on which to deal with people.

LIMA BEAN AND NUT CASSEROLE

Ingredients

1 onion, chopped
1 clove garlic, chopped up or squished
1 tbsp peanut oil (or similar)
14 oz chopped up tinned tomatoes
16 oz lima beans from a can, drained
4 oz unsalted peanuts
3/4 cups vegetable stock
2 tbsp peanut butter

Preparation

1. Whack the oven on to 350F.
2. Start frying the onion and garlic together in oil until brown.
3. Put this in a casserole bowl with tomatoes, beans and peanuts.
4. Stir the stock into the peanut lima and add to casserole, whilst stirring.
5. Cook in the oven for 40 minutes. Then eat.

—Ben Ayres, Cornershop

BRAZIL NUT ROAST EN CROUTE

Prepare a large oven tray by lining with parchment paper.

Pastry

1 lb puff pastry
soy milk to glaze

Nut Roast

2 large onions, peeled and chopped
1/4 cup vegan margarine
1 lb brazil nuts, finely grated
2 cups brown breadcrumbs
1/2 tsp dried thyme
3 tbsp lemon juice
salt and freshly ground black pepper
    (to taste)
a pinch of grated nutmeg, ground
    cloves and ground cinnamon
4 tbsp white wine or stock to mix, or
    enough to hold the roast together

Stuffing

2 cups brown breadcrumbs
2 tbsp chopped parsley
grated rind of 1 lemon and 1 tbsp of the juice
1 tsp each of dried thyme & dried marjoram
1/3 cup vegan margarine

Preparation

1. Heat the oven to 400°F.
2. Fry the onion in the margarine for 10 minutes until soft but not browned.
3. Remove from the heat and add the rest of the nut roast ingredients.
4. Make the stuffing by mixing all of the ingredients together to make a soft mixture.
5. Roll the pastry out on a floured board to a rectangle 2 x 14". Then place it on the prepared oven tray
6. Form the stuffing into a sausage about 10 in. Place this down the middle of the pastry.
7. Pile the nut roast mixture all over the stuffing including both ends.
8. Fold the ends of the pastry to enclose the mixture and stuffing, then bring both sides up and join on the top. Make the join an attractive frill. Brush the top and sides with soy milk.
9. Bake for 30 minutes until crisp.

"Sometimes I freeze before cooking and remove it from the freezer the night before required."
    —*Ita West Cussens, Cottage Vegan Guest House*

LIFE BUT HOW TO LIVE IT + DIRT + ONION BREATH + FEMALE HERCULES
MULLIGAN'S, MARCH 8, 1993

Life, But How to Live It? were from Norway and were hoping to play the same night as **Dirt**, from England, who Deko was bringing over to play in Mulligan's. It made sense to get both bands to play on the same bill. They were the only Norwegian band that we brought over. It's strange to note that more American bands came over than their mainland European counterparts. We never turned a band down because of their nationality. I think European bands aren't that concerned about playing Ireland or Britain. Their link to the country isn't as strong in many cases.

Mulligan's was a good venue that doubled up as a rehearsal/recording space as well as a venue. It was a little off the beaten track and sometimes this put people off going to the bands there. Its location proved a big factor in swaying neutrals not to go to gigs. This was and continues to be a shame and a problem.

Radioactive was a pirate radio station broadcasting from near Mulligan's. Hope got a show on it. It provided a forum for bands and people. It gave people a chance to hear what bands sounded like before going to their gig.

The evacuation procedure for Radioactive was very interesting. It involved a number of steps, including throwing the antennae to a certain place and then explaining to the authorities that you were practising at being a DJ. Licensing laws for broadcasting in Ireland are quite strict and are enforced in waves. Radioactive was caught up in one of those waves but managed to avoid prosecution. It provided a great service, including interviewing bands like **Life, But How To Live It?**

DOWN BY LAW + WHEEL + GROUNDSWELL
BARNSTORMERS, MAY 10, 1993

The singer from **Down By Law**, Dave Smalley, was very funny. "Hello Dublin. This is for all you **Thin Lizzy** fans out there," he shouted. We all looked up; most of us said, "Who?"

It was ironic that he was genuinely happy to be in the city where Phil Lynnot was born. I hadn't the heart to say he used to rehearse near my Mam's house and that the neighbours gave out stink about the noise.

At times we were like tourist guides for the country when bands travelled over. Mostly, though, it seemed that those who didn't live on the island knew more about its traditions. For those of us who were living in Dublin, the Book of Kells (for example) was just there. It didn't matter what it looked like because it would still be there tomorrow.

American bands always seemed to attract bigger crowds. Maybe it was because they had made a bigger effort to get over here. Dave Smalley used to be in **Dag Nasty** and **All** so he had some serious credentials that people wanted to check out.

SCRAMBLED TOFU

Ingredients:

16 oz package extra firm or firm tofu
2 tsp turmeric
1/2 tsp thyme
3 tbsp olive oil
salt and pepper to taste

Preparation

1. First, cut tofu into cubes. Put into medium mixing bowl and with a fork mash until crumbly.
2. Add spices and oil; mix well.
3. Heat medium frying pan on medium-high.
4. Toss in tofu and stir ocassionally until heated through, about 7 minutes.
5. Transfer to plate and serve with vegan bacon and waffles, if desired.

— *Carlos, Down By Law*

BRAWL | THE ATTIC, AUG. 25, 1993

I remember talking to Murt for the first time and being really excited by what he was trying to do in New Ross, a small country town in Wexford. He wanted bands to go there and play. He could get a venue and a PA and his band could also play.

Immediately we started telling bands about it and New Ross became a favourite for many people.

Unfortunately it petered out as people grew older and moved away. For two summers, though, anything was possible for the New Ross folk and it inspired many others around the southeast of Ireland.

POTATO CUBERS

Ingredients

2 potatoes, peeled, washed, and cubed
1 onion, chopped
4 big cloves of garlic, chopped
1 zucchini, peeled and sliced into long strips

Preparation

1. Heat oil and add cubed spuds; they tend to stick so keep an eye on them.
2. Add onions and garlic next and then the zucchinis.

It should look crispy and taste tangy. Add black pepper and mixed herbs if that's your thing. At four o'clock in the morning in the summer of 1993 this tasted like manna from heaven and Dawson liked it so that's OK with me. The advantages — cheap, fast and low fat. The disadvantages —cheap, fast and low fat.

"This recipe is more a spud thing than a vegan thing. Its first public outing was when we had Dawson (Glasgow) staying down with us in Ballykelly. I call it cubers.

The things I remember most about Hope are the friend-ships and the experiences. I can recall the gigs: having my head blown off by Nomeansno and not a drug in sight; meeting Steve from Arnheim and not being scared; Mini Buses from New Ross and stale biscuits; Brawl's van stuffed with people and cheap tobacco coming from Cork to a Fugazi gig in Dublin; learning the simplicity of doing it for ourselves and the warm feeling that gigs in small towns for small money were possible. All you had to do was ask and beg or borrow a PA system that didn't sound like a marching band in an empty Tayto bag. (Tayto is a brand of Crisps, also known as Potato Chips, in Ireland.–Ed.)

From a band point of view it has to be playing with Alice Donut (Dublin) and Jawbreaker (in Belfast). Seeing Flexihead for the first time still makes me feel kinda good. Knowing that music doesn't have to about who you know but what you feel. I probably won't ever see most of the people I met down through the years playing and putting on gigs (inspired by Hope). And it doesn't matter. It doesn't matter because it stays real and it remains unique. We all were, at one stage or another, a community of sorts. One other thing: To those from Kilkenny, Belfast, Derry, Portrush, Cork, Dublin, Netherlands, Belgium, France, Germany, Switzerland, Prague, Pilzen and the USA—Thanks."

—Murt Flynn, Brawl

HOLY ROLLERS | BARNSTORMERS, SEPT. 6, 1993

After putting on **Fugazi** four times it was nice to see another band from their label, Dischord records (based in Washington DC), coming over to Ireland. Tons of American bands were touring Europe and some, in turn, were getting to visit Ireland.

Many British bands were unhappy with their position. They had a shorter distance to travel and were willing to come over but they would still struggle greatly to attract a decent crowd. Bands seemed to be taken more seriously by Irish audience if they originated in the States. I think it may have something to do with the fact that bands have to go out of their way to travel over from the States so they are more appreciated. I hope that's what it is.

React was now a bi-monthly publication and I was struggling with it. It had become an expected part of the Dublin scene. People were waiting for its release and voicing their objection if it was "late." I set myself up for it as I aspired for it to be a monthly newsletter but the enjoyment was going from it. It became a sporadic publication after this issue and had lost any spark it may have had. With hindsight it would have been better to stop it now instead of it petering out like it did. I guess I wanted somebody else to do it.

BAKED RUTABAGA

Ingredients

1 large rutabaga (approx. 1 1/4 lbs), sliced thickly
1/6 cup margarine
2 onions, sliced
sage leaves
1 sprig rosemary
veg stock to cover

Preparation

1. Preheat the oven to 400°F. Line a baking dish or roasting can with a generous amount of margarine.
2. Lay the rutabaga and onion on the dish.
3. Season with salt and pepper and dash the sage and rosemary on top.
4. Lightly pour the stock so it just about covers the veg, then dot on the rest of the marg.
5. Bake in the oven for an hour, turning the swede over from time to time.

"Some people call turnips swedes. It is the vegetable that most Irish mothers seem to cook with pork chops and one that they must boil forever and ever before it's cooked. Generally I hate it, along with parsnips. The only way I can eat either veg is to bake them in the oven"

—*Niall, Hope Collective*

GOLDEN MILE + FLEXIHEAD + IN MOTION + GROUNDSWELL
BARNSTORMERS, OCT. 8, 1993

IN MOTION CURRY

Ingredients

2 eggplants
3 tbsp Garam Masala
2 bell peppers
3 tbsp cumin
2 onions
handful fresh cilantro
2 zucchini
8 leaves fresh basil
6 chilis
4 cloves garlic
2 sweet potatoes
1/2 cup tomato paste
1 tbsp ginger
4 cups vegetable stock
1 tbsp fennel seeds
2 cans coconut milk

Preparation

1. Sweat onions in large frying pan.
2. Add fennel seeds, garlic, ginger and chilis.
3. Reduce heat and add zucchini, eggplants and bell peppers.
4. Cook for 1 minute and then add cumin, Garam Masala and tomato paste.
5. Pour in veg stock and reduce by half.
6. Lastly, put in coconut milk, sweet potatoes, basil and cilantro.
7. Simmer for 20 minutes.
8. If needed, thicken with cornstarch.

"You may accompany this dish with a bag of chips from the local chippy and a slice of batch loaf bread. To garnish neatly arrange Tayto crisps around the edge of the plate. To finish 2 spoonfuls of Milk of Magnesia."
—Liam and John, In Motion

I distributed the *Statement* 12" by trading copies with people around the world who did their own 'zines and records. I then sold on their stuff at gigs. One of the people I traded with was involved in organising a day of awareness called "Stop The Madness" and had put together a compilation LP featuring **The Ex** amongst others. The latest idea was to have a number of benefit gigs in different cities around the world on the same day.

This was to help raise awareness about events in former Yugoslavia. Unfortunately, not too many people from Dublin came to show solidarity that night. **Golden Mile** had made the trip down from Belfast and were helped out by three other local bands but people just stayed home this evening.

Our gig had a live link with Sarajevo TV. They were due to ring the venue at 11 pm and in true Eurovision style I had to announce how much money was raised by the "Irish jury."

The phone was in the main bar and the venue was in a room behind it. When I was asked from Sarajevo how the gig was going I had to try and drown out the Barnstormer jukebox that was going full pelt in the background.

I hadn't the heart to say "There's no-one here, we've made no money—hope you're not too bummed out by this." Instead I made some excuses and avoided a direct answer. That night I became a politician. Me and Bono, eh?

NEUROSIS + PINCHER MARTIN + FRANK SIDEBOTTOM
BARNSTORMERS, NOV. 5 1993 | NOV. 11, 1993

Nineteen-ninety-three was a slow year for Hope in comparison to the previous one. We put on 14 gigs as well as being involved in getting bands to play in Cork, New Ross and Belfast.

We still hadn't got a suitable building for the café/venue. We had received sanction for grants for the co-op and had looked at many places. We came very close to getting one or two.

And then Jim from Cork asked us to help out with Frank Sidebottom. Enough to cheer anyone up.

How can one describe Frank? He's the one with the papier-mache head who sings songs about football and his home town of Timperley. He takes classic pop songs and gives them the Frank Sidebottom touch (hence Mull of Timperley, to the tune of Mull of Kintyre). In short, he's funny.

Not many get the joke and tonight's crowd was the worst we had had for a gig since **Babydigger** in the New Inn. I expected more of an interest. Frank had appeared on TV, had quite a few records out and enjoyed his share of music press coverage as well as producing *Oink* comic.

Maybe we didn't tell the right people. Ten people paid in. It was sad. Jim lost a fortune. He got loads of posters printed up and he had to pay for the venue. At least he enjoyed himself and there was a bigger crowd in Cork the next night.

TOMATO + ORANGE SOUP

Ingredients

2 onions chopped
1 clove of garlic, chopped finely—add more if you want
2 cans tomatoes
2 cups water/stock
basil
oregano
3 oranges

Preparation

1. Fry onion and garlic in some oil.
1. Pour tomatoes into a pot and add the water.
2. Boil and then simmer.
3. Grate the oranges and add it to the soup.
4. Cut up the orange and add it to the mix.
4. Add basil and oregano.

—Gary, Pincher Martin, Ciunas,
and Great Western Squares

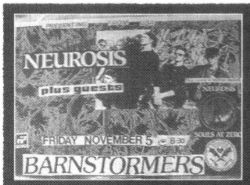

OI POLLOI | BARNSTORMERS, NOV. 21, 1993

This was a wild gig. **Oi Polloi** were a very political band and between songs, Deek was talking about many issues, issues that probably weren't spoken about too much at Hope gigs. A lot of the bands we had put on were political but preferred not to be too outspoken with their views. **Oi Polloi** were the complete opposite.

CHOCOLATE CUPCAKES WITH CHOCOLATE GANACHE FROSTING

Ingredients + Preparation

3 cups unbleached white flour
2 cups sugar
2/3 cups cocoa powder
2 tsp baking soda
1 tsp salt

Into a bowl add:
2 cups cold water
1/2 cup plus 2 tablespoons vegetable oil
2 tsp vanilla extract
2 tbsp lemon juice or apple cider vinegar

Then:
1. Pour the liquid ingredients into the dry ingredients and blend well with a big whisk. Beat out all of the lumps.
2. Using a ladle, spoon the batter into cupcake trays, filling them about 3/4 full (just about to the top). If you don't use cupcake papers, make sure to oil the tray really well and dust with cocoa powder so the cupcakes don't stick. I use a giant tray for 12 cupcakes and usually have enough batter left over to make another tiny cake or to let folks lick it up.
3. Bake at 350°F. After about 30 minutes test the centers with a toothpick or cake tester (a small knife would also do the trick). If the tester comes out clean

they are done. Cool for ten minutes, then turn out cupcakes to cool fully.

GANACHE FROSTING

Ingredients

1 bar vegan chocolate
rice or soy milk
shredded coconut

Preparation

1. Place the chocolate in a bowl over a pot with some water in it over medium heat to get the water to steam.
2. Stir the chocolate until it melts smooth.
3. Pour a very small amount of milk into the chocolate and keep stirring vigorously. At first the chocolate will sort of curd up, but if you keep stirring it quickly a smooth consistency develops.
4. Immediately turn off the heat. After a few minutes spoon the chocolate over cooled muffins and allow the chocolate to set about 15 minutes.
5. Sprinkle the tops with coconut or add more chocolate chips. Leave to cool, preferably in the fridge.

—Niall, Hope Promotions

HERB GARDEN | FOX + PHEASANT, DEC. 1, 1993

PAPRIKASH

A stew that works great with dumplings.

Ingredients

1 large onion, sliced
3 cloves garlic, chopped (optional)
2 carrots sliced
2 potatoes peeled and diced
1 red bell pepper sliced
1 yellow bell pepper, sliced
some cooked beans or fried tofu
1 carton/bottle sieved tomatoes
some bay leaves
2 tbsp paprika
1 stock cube
salt and pepper to taste
oil for frying

Preparation

1. Heat the oil in a pan and sauté the onions and garlic until soft. Add in carrots and potatoes and cook for 10 minutes.
2. Put in paprika, bay leaves and pepper. Stir well and sauté for about 2–3 minutes so that the peppers are coated in some oil and paprika.
3. Add the sieved tomatoes, beans, stock cube and enough boiling water so that everything is covered in liquid.
4. Simmer for 15 minutes. Serve with some soy yoghurt or some soy dream and lemon juice.

—Suzy, Warzone

GINGERED CARROT SOUP

Ingredients

2 garlic cloves
1 piece fresh ginger (approx. 1 in)
3/4 lb carrots (about 10 carrots)
1 cup red lentils
juice of 2 oranges
3 cups vegetable stock
5 parsley sprigs
10 cilantro sprigs
1 lime/lemon
oil for frying

Preparation

1. Chop garlic and ginger and fry gently for 10 minutes in olive oil.
2. Chop and add the parsley.
3. Scrape and chop the carrots in small pieces. Add the chopped carrots, the orange juice, the lentils and the vegetable stock to the pan.
4. Bring to boil, then cover, and let the mixture simmer on a low heat for 15–20 minutes.
5. Purée the soup (if possible) in a blender or a food-processor.
6. Serve with a slice of lime/lemon and a firm hand of chopped coriander.
(Add salt and freshly ground pepper to taste.)

—Pim, Revenge Of The Carrots

GAN + THE REVS | THE ATTIC, DEC. 20, 1993

PASTA SALAD

Ingredients

pasta
TVP or soy chunks
1 red bell pepper
1 small onion
some lettuce
vegan mayonnaise
soy sauce
1 small can corn
salad dressing (French style)

Preparation

1. Soak some TVP chunks in boiling water—add a couple of spoons of gravy mix for extra flavour.
2. When rehydrated, drain off the liquid and marinade the chunks in a mixture of soy sauce and salad dressing for at least an hour.
3. Then fry the chunks until they go brown.
4. Boil the pasta and rinse it in cold water, then put it in a big bowl.
5. Chop the red bell pepper, onion, and lettuce and mix into the pasta, adding the fried TVP chunks.
6. Drain the liquid from the corn and throw it in too. Mix together with a couple of spoons of vegan mayo.
7. Keep it in the fridge until you decide to mash it all down your hairy gullet and then fall asleep in the garden with your beverage of choice.

"Love, peace, & pasta shapes."

—Dave, GAN + One Car Pile Up

The **Revs** were the closest thing to a mod band that Hope put on. They were immaculately dressed and played music reminiscent of the 1979 mod scene that had spawned bands like **Secret Affair**, **Squire**, and **Purple Hearts**.

We weren't expecting much of a crowd so The Attic was a more suitable option as a venue. We decided not to just use Barnstormers, as small crowds made the place seem too big.

Sometimes there's just no guessing how many people will show to a gig. It depends on many factors like other options available to people on the night, choice of venue, other bands on the bill.

We took a gamble that no more than 100 people would want to share an evening five days before Christmas with **Gan** or **The Revs**. It was the right choice for us but it was a great night.

Hopes' gig year ended with this event in The Attic and still no regular all-ages venue to do stuff in. That was the dream. Now to try and make it happen in 1994.

LUNGFISH + CIRCUS LUPUS + FLEXIHEAD | BARNSTORMERS, FEB. 22, 1994

Daniel Higgis, the singer from **Lungfish**, was an imposing character. He spoke little and the words that came out took a while to make sense to the listener. Radioactive did an interview with Daniel on the night of the gig. Talking to the DJ later, he said it was the best interview he'd ever done. When I asked him why, he replied, "That dude has some whacked-out ideas."

Lungfish and **Circus Lupus** on the same bill whetted many people's appetites and having **Flexihead** open proceedings made it an even more exciting evening. The fact that two bands were on Dischord records ensured that there was a large attendance at the gig. Few were disappointed.

APPLE CORNBREAD

Ingredients

2 apples, peeled and chopped thinly

1 1/2 cup unbleached white flour

1 1/2 cup blue corn meal (or regular yellow corn meal)

3 1/2 tsp baking soda

1/2 tsp salt

1 tbsp Sucanat (Described as unrefined natural sugar made from evaporated sugar cane juice—*Ed.*)—brown sugar will work fine, though

2 1/4 cup vanilla soymilk

1 tsp cinnamon

1/4 cup apple sauce

2 tbsp maple syrup

Preparation

1. Preheat oven to 400°F.
2. In a large bowl, combine all ingredients except the apple.
3. Mix in the apple. Do not overmix as the bread could become tough.
4. Bake 35–45 minutes on the top shelf of the oven.
5. Bread is done when an inserted knife comes out clean, about 40 minutes.

—*Asa Osborne, Lungfish*

HOPE MEMORIES PART 2

What with putting up Hope bands, *React*, *Gearhead Nation*, Catharsis, Radioactive and various (more or less short lived) record and zine distros, myself, Niall and Miriam became good friends. After they decided to stop doing Hope promotions Niall continued to write to do other stuff—contributing to GN, writing *Wide* and *No Way Referee* (two football fanzines), shows on Radioactive etc. >>

CHAPTER FOUR

dawning of a new era?

"Around 1996 we were both complaining to each other about the way gigs were being done in Dublin. The climate had changed from a kind of excitement to play and be part of something to a more "professional" attitude, although even now I have the nagging feeling that "professionalism" was used to disguise a more insidious money/ego trip. Looking back I can understand how bands wanted different things, the problem was that often what came across was a "the world owes us" attitude, from some local, as well as international groups. It was only a minority of people but it really sucked the energy out of the thing.

The thing that had always attracted me to Hope and the D.I.Y. way of doing things was that it was the meeting ground between music and politics. Every gig was an act of opposition to the commodification of music and it seemed important that the people who didn't want to collaborate with major labels and money-hungry promoters should have the choice. My interest had always been turned towards this opposition—the resistance to corporate rule over cultural values.

One of the core ideas of Hope and the reason the other projects existed was a simple idea—don't just complain about things, do something to change them. So we began to talk about restarting something similar to Hope, but this time in a collective form—different people expressed interest and, the then-untitled Hope Collective was born. We refused to work with major labels or their bands because of their links to multinational corporations, who directly or indirectly participate in human rights abuses everywhere. We wanted to nourish something different to this, an idea built around mutual respect and independence. Whether or not we did a good job is open to discussion.

THE THING THAT HAD ALWAYS ATTRACTED ME TO HOPE AND THE DO IT YOURSELF WAY OF DOING THINGS WAS THAT IT WAS THE MEETING GROUND BETWEEN MUSIC AND POLITICS.

I always associate the Collective meetings with food—tea, coffee, biscuits—and table football in the flat on Blessington Street. It's important to note that the first question was always, "Do we want to see the band? Do we want to put them on? When? Where?" Money never came into it for us—the idea of no guarantees wasn't to avoid having to pay bands—we always fed, housed and paid bands from abroad as a priority, local bands when we could—the idea was to cultivate a different atmosphere where the bands trusted us to look after them.

Maybe it would have been better to give bands a minimum guarantee so they were sure they weren't going to be losing money (even though we knew they weren't). I think that attitude could have turned bands towards the "real promoters" who gave guarantees (usually at the expense of a hiked door price). After a while we decided to each contribute £1.50 or £2 to a kitty every week to build up a small reserve in case we needed it. I don't know if there was money left over or what happened to it. After the gigs we'd publish the accounts in *React* and then later in *Gearhead Nation* so everyone who came to the gigs knew where their money had gone. We'd make money on some gigs, lose money on others, but it always evened out. Free photocopying, appropriated sellotape, and Finbar and Pete's computers helped a lot.

The collective had a very loose structure where we decided things by consensus, with some of the most circular, drawn out discussions ever had, and some of the funniest ones too. I have a vague memory of one decision being decided on a game of table football. Financially it was pretty simple, we weren't officially registered with anybody so all money that came into the collective was used for gig expenses and to pay bands. No collective member ever got paid and frankly I don't think it ever crossed anybody's mind, not for the smallest second. We were really just happy to be doing things our own way, putting personal politics and a love of music into what we hoped was a collective party, where band, organizers, and audience all participated and the ubiquitous cult of personality had little bites taken out it of whenever possible." —Derek

CHEAPSKATE + BRIAN BANNON + STOMACH + GOUT + UNDERFOOT + NURSE DIESEL + JACKBEAST | THE ATTIC, MARCH 29 + APRIL 6, 1996 | HOPE COLLECTIVE BENEFITS

After we came back from Canada I was feeling pretty healthy and started working again. Since coming home no bands had asked about coming over. Timo and Leagues did some stuff when we were away and had decided to try and make a living from it. I never wanted to go down that road. For me it was a hobby, I didn't want to have to make decisions based purely on finance. Derek, from *Gearhead Nation*, asked if we would be interested in sharing our promotion experiences with some other people. He had been talking to some friends about doing gigs independently.

Pete O'Neill from Belfast had been in touch saying that **Bikini Kill**, **BIS** and **Team Dresch** wanted to come over. Gary from Wiija records was coordinating it and had asked for Hope to do the gig in Dublin. I met Johnny (who I contacted about the first **Fugazi** gig) at a **Rocket From The Crypt** gig. He was very complimentary about Hope and felt that it was a shame we were operating no longer. Other people had also lamented the absence of Hope, which was nice and made me think it may be time to get it going again.

After a bit of cajoling Mir and I decided to go along to a meeting in Derek's house. There were 12 of us: Cliona, Derek, Pete, Anto, Eugene, Mero, Dave, Clodagh, Jamie, Aoife, Miriam and I. From there the Hope Collective was born. We decided to pay optional weekly subs, £2 a week. We could then use the money to put on gigs or have a floating fund in reserve. We were all keen on putting on **BIS** and the others. Before that gig we thought it would be nice to organise a couple of benefits in The Attic. Our way of saying we are back. We would do a newsletter for the gig and give out some food (all vegan of course) as a welcoming present for people.

We'll forever be indebted to the bands for playing the benefits and many like them who gave their service for no monetary payment. It wasn't about finance though, was it? The gigs were a huge success with big crowds and great

HOPPIN' JOHN AKA CHEAPSKATE STEW

Ingredients

1/2 lb black-eyed peas, soaked overnight
4 cups water
1 1/2 cups good brown rice
a couple of onions
14 oz can or 8 fresh tomatoes
1/2 teaspoon cayenne pepper
a teaspoon or so salt (or large table-spoongood tamari sauce)
8 cloves crushed garlic
1 tbsp decent veggie oil
2 inch piece of kombu (kelp) if ya can steal it, or pay if yer rich

Preparation

1. Put beans and water in a big pot, open a bottle of good beer.
2. Add salt/tamari to beans, boil about 10 mins, simmer for an hour. Meanwhile roll a joint, have a smoke.
3. After 45 minutes, add rice, simmer 35–40 minutes.
4. Sauté onion/garlic 5 min. add rest of stuff, keep going for 5 more min.
5. Next ya just add it to the beans and rice. If ya can get kombu just throw it with the beans at the start, it might help you not fart so much.
6. Okay, after ya throw all together simmer yet again for 15–20 minutes, then it should all be done.

"This recipe comes from somewhere down past the blue ridge mountains and traditionally is served with corn-bread, but in Ireland it makes a great winter warming meal."

—*Burkie, Cheapskate*

BIS, BIKINI KILL, TEAM DRESCH | CHARLIE'S BAR, APRIL 20, 1996

One week after **BIS** appeared on "Top Of The Pops" they played Charlie's. Seemingly they were the first unsigned band on the show. The hype around today's gig was unreal. It was the one and only time a Hope gig was mentioned on the billboards around Dublin. It was listed as an "event of the month" on a generic beer company sponsored poster. We weren't happy with this. We were fuming for a number of reasons:

1) Hope was actively against using a company to advertise our gigs on pieces of wood splattered around our city, especially a company that has a monopoly on splattering.

2) Beer companies had no interest in supporting the Dublin music scene, only in achieving some recognition from it.

This gig started at 3pm to ensure that there would be no age restrictions at the door. This gig had nothing to do with a beer company, other than being hosted by a pub (an unfortunate but necessary circumstance).

Before the gig we spent 45 minutes removing Heineken banners draped throughout the venue. The owners thought we were insane. They couldn't understand our logic. It was truly awful.

It felt good to have Hope back doing a no age restrictions gig on a Saturday afternoon. **Bikini Kill** seemed like a valid reference for what we were doing. We were trying to encourage people to do things themselves and **Bikini Kill** were acting as role models for women to get involved in music.

CHILI NON CARNE

Ingredients

1/2 of a medium onion
1 clove garlic
1 cup soy hamburger
1 can chopped tomatoes (14 oz)
3/4 can kidney beans (12 oz)
1/2 bell pepper (red or green)
1 small can corn (approx. 6 oz)
1 tsp chili powder
1 tsp salt
1/2 tsp pepper
1/2 tsp cumin
1 tbsp oil
1 bag tortilla chips (4 oz)

Preparation

1. Heat the oil in a pot and sautée the onions and garlic until soft. Add the peppers and soy, mince and cook for another couple of minutes.
2. To this mixture add chili powder, pepper, cumin and salt. Mix thoroughly and then add the tomatoes and kidney beans (washed and drained).
3. Simmer for about ten minutes.
4. Readjust the spices to taste and add the corn (drained).
5. Cook for another couple of minutes and serve over the chips. Add jalepeños and vegan cheese on top if desired.

—Amanda, BIS

GAMEFACE + CLEANSLATE + BLOOD OR WHISKEY + PINCHER MARTIN DA CLUB, MAY 28, 1996

LONELY PLANET GIRL MUFFINS

Ingredients

1/2 cup canola oil
1/2 to 3/4 cup maple syrup
egg replacer for two eggs
1 tsp vanilla
1 1/2 cup grated carrots (2 large carrots)
1 cup grated zucchini (1-2 medium zucchini)
1 3/4 cup rice flour
1 tsp baking powder
1 tsp baking soda
1/2 tsp salt
1 1/2 to 2 tbsp allspice

Preparation

1. Preheat oven to 350°F
2. Mix wet stuff together well
3. Add carrots + zucchini (courgette) and all the rest, mixing just until blended. Lumps are OK.
4. Pour into greased muffin pans or one large loaf pan or 2 small loaf pans.
5. Bake muffins for about 25-30 minutes, about an hour for the bread, or until a knife comes out clean.

"These are the only kinds of treats I'm allowed to eat. Free of wheat, refined sugar, dairy. You can't go wrong. Go ORGANIC as much as possible. Buy local."

—Donna, Team Dresch

Ian from Meantime contacted us and asked if we would be interested in putting on **Gameface** from New York, who were touring with **Cleanslate** from the Czech Republic. He had asked some others from Ireland who weren't willing to take a risk on it.

We thought it would be nice to see a band from Eastern Europe playing in Dublin so we said yes. We had a problem getting a venue as The Attic was too small and Charlie's wasn't available. A new venue had just opened called the DA (Dublin Arts) club. We didn't think they'd want to put the gig on but they agreed after much cajoling from Pete.

The gig itself was a musically varied night in a cool venue. Highlight was probably sitting in cinema seats listening to the punked up traditional tunes of **Blood Or Whiskey**.

The DA club was a lovely venue and it was unfortunate that it lasted little over a year before becoming a clothes shop. It was small and on two floors but had a nice atmosphere. It was double-booked quite often and the management had an arrogant take on live music.

They did whatever they felt and seemed to pay little heed to the bands. They would leave people for days before making any decisions on whether the venue was available. They would rearrange bookings at short notice. Most people felt them unreliable. Such a pity it vanished.

LITHIUM JOE + CRANC + THE NORVICS | THE ATTIC, JUNE 29, 1996

POT NOODLES

Ingredients

1 tub of freeze-dried pot noodles
hot water

Preparation

1. Boil kettle
2. Pour contents of said kettle over collection of desiccated rats entrails, diced winos liver and dried peas passing itself off as ready meal.
3. Consume.
4. Head off somewhere interesting and truly live your life!!!!!!

"As for memories of the tour in Ireland. . . hell, I've got loads of fantastic memories from that time. Losing the van door in Dundalk, the drummer from the support band in Waterford who asked to borrow a stick cos he'd only brought one, dropping the goalposts on the shores of Galway Bay on Aidy's head (he's never been the same since), but most of all the hospitality and friendship of the people we met over there who were always welcoming and never once told us to feck off ... despite obvious provocation. The time of my life ... absolutely brilliant!!"

—Paul Thompson, Lithium Joe

Paul from Monaghan got in touch with me about putting bands on there. They wanted bands to travel and had a venue that would host them.

Lithium Joe were an English band who wanted to travel and play as many gigs as possible. They contacted me about coming over, so they played and visited Monaghan. Around this time Bobo from Dundalk was interested in doing stuff so they played and visited there also.

These places have popped up at various times, the problem is getting them to stay active. People tend to move on from smaller towns and the folk who were instrumental in organizing things don't stay around for ever. On the plus side, though, when smaller towns get bands travelling though the crowds are generally more appreciative. This in turn pleases the bands. Just ask **Lithium Joe**.

Jerome, from the band **Cranc**, was also involved in putting on gigs in Monaghan and he asked could they play this Dublin gig. **Cranc** sounded even poppier than the poppy **Lithium Joe** at their poppiest. But they still did stuff in their hometown, so how could we turn them down?

It was the start of a new cycle. Monaghan, Dundalk, Belfast and Dublin could all be played on concurrent days with little traveling. It suited bands who had the time to travel and play small gigs.

DES MAN DIABLO | THE ATTIC, AUG. 14, 1996

LEEK AND POTATO CASSEROLE

Ingredients

about 4 big potatoes
a leek
some chickpeas (as much as you want)
romaine lettuce
garlic (as much as you want)
vegetable stock

Preparation

1. Soak the chickpeas overnight.
2. Slice the potatoes fairly thickly. Put the chick peas in a pot with layers of potatoes on top of them. then boil them for about 30–40 minutes or until the chickpeas are cooked and the potatoes are pretty mushy.
3. Slice up the leek and chop up the garlic then fry them together in a bit of olive oil until the leek is a little softened.
4. Then put the the chickpeas, potatoes, garlic and leek together in a pot with some vegetable stock (as much as you want, depending on whether you want the soup/casserole thick or thin). bring to the boil and then simmer for about 20 minutes.
5. Add about a handful of sliced romaine lettuce and stir in.
6. There you go . . . and it's especially nice if you serve it with grated vegan cheese.

—Aoife O'Leary, Hope Collective

Des Man Diablo from England were playing Belfast and asked to come to Dublin. They were willing to do an afternoon gig in The Attic (who had tentatively agreed to the event). They were the first band I'd seen in years that all wore shoes—loafers and brogues but not a runner in sight.

THAI STYLE STIR FRY NOODLES

Ingredients

1 tbsp lemongrass (fresh)
3 red chilis (fresh)
1 onion finely chopped
1 tsp turmeric
1 1/3 cups coconut milk
1 small can bamboo shoots
7 oz baby corn
7 oz mushrooms
7 oz cauliflower or broccoli
1 red bell pepper
1 tbsp chopped fresh ginger
1/2 lb egg-free noodles

Preparation

1. Heat oil in a wok or pan. Add in onions and herbs. Cook for 2–3 minutes.
2. Add broccoli (or cauliflower), red bell pepper and corn and fry for 5 minutes.
3. Add coconut milk, bamboos shoots and mushrooms. Let simmer for 10 minutes.
4. Meanwhile cook noodles according to instrucions on packet (generally in boiling water for up to 5 minutes). Serve stir fry on noodles.

—Ebola

BULL TACO + FRANKIE STUBBS + BROODER + MONKHOUSE + BLUNT + CONSUME + RELAPSE + SEAN FORBES + CAPRATONE + THE SLIPPES + PET LAMB
CITY ARTS CENTRE, AUG. 15,16,17 | 1996 D.I.Y. FESTIVAL

Arising from our weekly Hope meetings and me bumping into Alison, who worked in the City Arts Centre, talk of a festival surfaced. Alison said the City Arts Centre would be interested in co-promoting such a thing and asked for our suggestions.

We spoke about it at length and felt it would be good to have workshops on how to do your own fanzine, how to bring out your own record, and even on how to put on a gig. We thought it would be interesting to have a discussion on independent music in Dublin. Alison invited Pat O'Mahoney from RTE Television to act as devil's advocate at that discussion. She was able to get money from the management of the Arts Centre (which in turn is funded by the Arts Council).

This meant we needn't worry about meeting a band's travel expenses. **Bull Taco**, featuring Frankie Stubbs from **Leatherface** was looking to play that weekend so we invited them. We also got Sean from **Wat Tyler** to come over as a speaker. Sean's label Rugger Bugger had been involved in doing things independently for years. We got bands from outside Dublin to play. **Consume**, **Monkhouse** and **Brooder** all traveled for the festival and got their expenses met.

The only condition from City Arts people was that they asked a couple of bands AND they had suggestions for some workshops. We were fine

VEGAN PANCAKES

Ingredients

1 potato

Preparation

Frantically stab a potato with a fork and put it in the oven for one hour (for a medium sized pot), for fan assisted oven make allowances. Take it out and scoff it with some mock beef jerky.

—Frankie Stubbs, Leatherface + Jesse

by this, as we were not questioned on our activities.

It was pretty successful. People absorbed a ton of information as various organizations were invited to set up stalls. Sean gave out information on a record pressing plant in the Czech Republic that wasn't expensive to use. A lot of Irish bands have since given that company business. The gigs had no age restrictions and many people went to the workshops. The music was pretty much secondary but **Frankie Stubbs'** solo performance of "Not Superstitious" with that gravel voice was amazing.

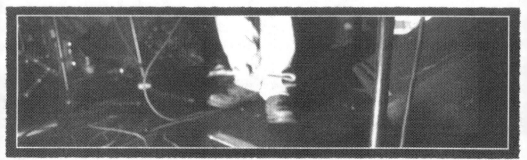

POLARIS + LORETTA + JACKBEAST | THE ATTIC, SEPT. 6, 1996

BASSETTI'S TABBOULEH SALAD

Ingredients

1 to 1 1/2 cups presoaked couscous/bulgur wheat
2 cups fresh parsley finely chopped
1/2 cup fresh mint chopped
2 large or 3 small tomatoes finely chopped
3 large or 4 small cucumbers peeled and
    finely chopped
handful of fresh garden peas
1/4 to 1/3 cup lemon juice
salt and pepper to taste
fresh pressed garlic (to taste)
pita bread
vinaigrette or light textured Italian style dressing

Preparation

1. Use a large mixing bowl and mix together pre-soaked couscous/bulgar wheat
with just enough dressing to moisten.
2. Add chopped parsley, mint, tomato,
cucumber and peas. If you use an elec-
tric chopper for the tomato and cucumber, they will be mostly juice and pulp.
This is acceptable for a softer salad,
however you will get better results from
hand chopping, though this can be
quite time consuming.
3. Add the lemon juice, salt, pepper, and
garlic to taste. Cover and chill salad for
at least two hours . . . it needs time to
soak in it's own juices to really bring
out the flavour of all the ingredients.

*"Serve with hummus and warm pita bread. The salad
will be quite juicy at the bottom of the bowl. Do not
remove the juice, as it acts as a marinade, the longer it
soaks, the better the flavor."*

—Bassetti, Jackbeast

The City Arts Centre was available to
hire as a venue but it proved really expensive. It had no PA and Arts Centre staff had
to be paid. You would need at least 100
people paying in to a gig to break even on
the venue before worrying about getting
money for the bands.

With that in mind we went for The
Attic (at £40) when **Polaris** from Leeds
asked to come over. It left us with the con-
tinuing problem of getting people into the
gigs who were under 18, a problem that still
needs amending.

Jackbeast were a great band. They
rehearsed in the City Centre. If ever we
needed any equipment for a gig we could
always ask them and they would oblige. It
was refreshing to deal with a band like that.
I'm not sure they got the recognition they
should have.

DOWN BY LAW | THE ATTIC, SEPT. 13, 1996

Back again for more reminiscing about Phil Lynnott, only this time they played in The Attic. I was amazed by people's reaction to **Down By Law**. It seemed so negative. They attracted pretty small crowds yet they were on a pretty big label, wrote some great songs and had a "name" within the "scene." It was unfortunate yet we lost money both times **Down By Law** played in Ireland.

TOBI'S CARROT SALAD FOR XMAS DINNER

Ingredients

4 cups of carrots, grated
1 cup of parsley, chopped

Preparation

1. Mix grated organically grown carrots with organically grown chopped parsley.
2. Chill and serve.
3. If you like you can make an oil and vinegar dressing and pour about 1/4 cup of this on the salad before you chill.

—Tobi Vail, Bikini Kill

VEGAN TAPENADE

Ingredients

10 oz kalamata olives
1/4—1/2 virgin olive oil (depending on taste)
1-2 fat green chilis
3 cloves garlic
bunch of cilantro
splash of apple juice concentrate
1 small lemon juiced
some ground black pepper (to taste)
Note: do not add salt!

Preparation

1. Roughly chop all ingredients then whizz them to a paste with a hand blender.

"Spread on homemade wholewheat bread/oatcakes or mix with veg and pasta /in pita bread with salad. This is very rich so use sparingly. It lasts up to a week."

—Rosa, Steve and Romy, Newcastle

CITIZEN FISH + DYSFUNCTIONAL + CHEAPSKATE
CHARLIE'S, SEPT. 26, 1996

RED HOT SPAGHETTI

Ingredients

spaghetti
plenty of olive oil for frying
1 clove garlic (or more to taste)
pesto sauce
tomato paste
peanut butter
soy sauce
marmite
seaweed
herbs
chili sauce

Preparation

1. Boil water, cook spaghetti.
2. Meanwhile, slowly heat a LOT of olive oil in a frying pan, and add a clove or two of finely sliced garlic.
3. Mix up all or some of the following in quantities to taste: red/green pesto, tomato paste, peanut butter, soy sauce, marmite, seaweed, herbs and the redhot bit, which for the purposes of mindrushing after-effects, should ideally be Dave's Insanity Sauce—it's extremely hot and a few drops makes all the difference (a bottle can last for months), or green thai curry paste (check theres no fish in the ingredients) or chilis.
4. Chuck all that in the pan and stir.
5. Drain the spaghetti.
6. Mix the sauce into the spaghetti for an all-through-the-meal consistency.

"Coffee highlights the burn/rush, and it all takes less than 20 minutes!"

—*Dick Lucas, Citizen Fish*

Wow! Charlie's was packed for this one. It was the ideal venue. Even though it was quite big, the stage was nonexistent and you could have afternoon gigs with no age restrictions.

However, when the crowd got moving the whole floor shook and the PA could get quite a whalloping. The PA was on two stands and it was in danger of falling whenever people got too excited. This was fine if there were some people around to hold on to it. If not there was every chance of it falling down. There were a few of us holding on to the PA for dear life that night.

The first time I saw Dick Lucas in a band was in 1984 when **Subhumans** played Ireland with **Shrapnel**, **Golden Horde**, **Paranoid Visions** and **Vicarious Living** (oh and **Cactus World News**) over two nights in the Youth Expression Centre in Temple Bar. Here in Charlie's 12 years and two bands later he had changed little—still belting out great songs and still dealing in lyrics that meant something to him and hopefully to others in the crowd. He is an inspiration for sure.

LOS CRUDOS + HOLO-CHRIST + EBOLA + RELAPSE | THE ATTIC, OCT. 16, 1996

This gig was full of surprises. It was totally packed (coming during a trough in gig-going for many people) and the attention people paid during the songs was unusual.

One could hear the proverbial dropping of a pin during **Los Crudos** singer Martin's onstage introductions. No doubt the bar staff in The Attic were glad of the break, however I'm sure the management were amazed.

Generally speaking, in between songs is a time when liquid refreshments are ordered. Not so tonight. We were too busy hearing about worldwide injustices to worry about ordering alcohol.

Tonight's gig was an indiction that politics and music do mix and the problems in Chiapas in Mexico that were highlighted by **Los Crudos** tonight were taken on board by people afterwards.

TORTA FRITA / FRY BREAD

Ingredients

2 cups flour
1 tsp baking powder
1 tsp baking soda
1 tbsp salt
warm water (mixed with soy milk if you wish)
oil for frying

Preparation

1. Mix dry ingredients together—add in water and mix well until the dough is not sticking to your fingers. If it's too wet add more flour.
2. Heat oil—make sure it's very hot. Rip off pieces of the dough and smooth it out a bit with your hand.
3. Fry dough until it's golden brown.
4. You can add sweeteners like syrup, sugar and cinnamon or eat it like regular bread.
4. Great for cold rainy days.

—Los Crudos

DROP DEAD + NECKWEED + JACKBEAST | THE ATTIC, NOV. 5, 1996

One month on from **Los Crudos** and just as noisy, **Drop Dead** were another political band who played extremely heavy music. The sort of music that ensures all lyrics need an explanation, as they are impossible for the listener to decipher.

If we had our way we would have asked **Jackbeast** to play every Hope gig. It certainly wasn't fair and we tried not to ask them each time. Tonight was one of the nights we could squeeze them in and again they were memorable.

Neckweed were the first band from Carlow to play a Hope gig. Following on from activity in New Ross, they were part of the growing band of people from the Southeast who were interested in doing things.

KUNG FU RAMEN

Ingredients

good brand Szechuan stir fry sauce
unsalted shelled peanuts
4–6 packs of ramen (noodles—check
    that they're veggie)
I can of water chestnuts
broccoli
I red bell pepper
I green bell pepper
scallions
Chinese cabbage
bamboo shoots
tofu
oil for frying

Preparation

1. Cut up all veggies and stir-fry in oil with tofu.
2. Add peanuts and Szechuan sauce.
3. Boil ramen and drain.
4. Mix ramen and veggies. Serve.

—*Bob, Drop Dead*

PUNKROCK EGGPLANT

Ingredients

4 big eggplants
I clove garlic
5 tbsp olive oil
I tbsp freshly squeezed lemon juice
2 tbsp fresh, chopped thyme
I tsp minced white pepper
I 1/2 lbs tomatoes (1/2 in slices)
6 oz vegan cheese (large slices)

Preparation

1. Cut the eggplant in 1/2 in. slices lengthwise but let it "hang" together by the end (where the leaf is). Put in a ovenproof dish and put salt on the surfaces. Leave it for 15 min.
2. Chop garlic and mix with the oil, lemon juice, thyme and the pepper.
3. Wipe the salt from the eggplant and put the tomatoes in between the eggplant slices.
4. Pour the spice oil over the eggplants with a spoon and stick the slices of cheese in between.
5. Warm at the bottom at 425°F for approx. 25 minutes.
6. Serve with bread.

— *Champ, Astream*

STOMACH + BAMBI + CHEAPSKATE + BLACKBELT JONES + JACKBEAST + STEAM PIG + PORN + BRIAN BANNON + YAWN | THE ATTIC, DEC. 7 + 13, 1996 BENEFITS FOR SIMON COMMUNITY + RATHMINES WOMEN'S REFUGE

For the first Christmas as the Hope Collective we decided to do a couple of benefits. Christmas always seems a time when organisations that look after some less fortunate people receive a bit more attention.

I am not a great believer in charity gigs as I don't believe they change the root of the problems. A lot of voluntary groups would not be neccessary if more concerted efforts were made at a political level.

The Simon Community feed, homeless people and the Rathmines Women's Refuge houses women who have been abused. Both organizations need a lot more help than we could dream of giving them from a benefit gig. However, it is a token gesture and at least shows a certain solidarity with the people involved and affected.

Admission for the Simon gig was £2 or perishable food items worth at least that value. For the other gig it was £2 or toys to that value. At the end of both gigs there were sacks of goods going to the groups as well as some money. They were both sucessful in the regard that they raised money/some awareness.

Unfortunately the need for both organizations still exists today, now more than ever.

LIBERATION BEANS

Ingredients

10 mushrooms (more, or less to taste), chopped
1 large onion, chopped
4 large pre-boiled potatoes, chopped
vegetable oil
can of baked beans, drained
beer (optional)
1 cup curry sauce; please check your sauce for veganicity
jacks roll (plenty of)*

Preparation

1. Preheat large pan with very liberal amount of the oil.
2. Add mushrooms, onion, potatoes to the pan, ensuring that the pan is at a fairly high heat.
3. Stir fry for approx 5–6 min. or until things start to brown up.
4. Add the curry sauce and beans and allow to simmer away for about 10 minutes and then serve.
5. Beer is highly recommended as an accompaniment to this dish. (Jacks roll becomes self-explanatory).

"I have been assured that the dish has as much nutritional value as 20 John Player Blue but is a nice change to the norm . . . ENJOY."

—Wally, Stomach

(For those not completely familiar with the Dublin dialect, "Jacks roll" goes under the pseudonym of toilet roll in other English-speaking cities. —Ed.)

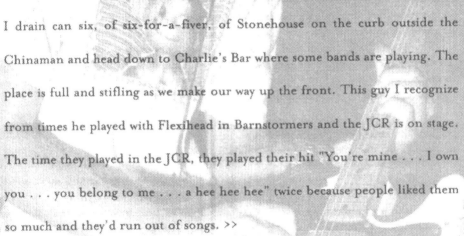

I drain can six, of six-for-a-fiver, of Stonehouse on the curb outside the

Chinaman and head down to Charlie's Bar where some bands are playing. The

place is full and stifling as we make our way up the front. This guy I recognize

from times he played with Flexihead in Barnstormers and the JCR is on stage.

The time they played in the JCR, they played their hit "You're mine . . . I own

you . . . you belong to me . . . a hee hee hee" twice because people liked them

so much and they'd run out of songs. >>

CHAPTER 5
new beginnings

"The band he's in tonight is **Jackbeast**, still my favorite band ever to come out of Dublin. I remember coming away from every **Jackbeast** gig feeling completely overcome with emotion, almost crying. I'd come to this gig hoping to talk to someone about getting a show for the band I was in at the time, the **Null Set**, and was thrown towards Derek Byrne. He was on his haunches watching **Jackbeast** when I spoke to him for the first time. I went to hand him a tape we'd made. Dazed, he turned towards me, biting his lip, perspiring slightly and motioned to me that something was stopping him from speaking to me until after **Jackbeast** had finished; he'd experienced it before but didn't think it necessary to articulate.

When the show was finished, he took the tape from me and told me he'd be in touch soon. He seemed like a nice guy, really enthusiastic. I think within a couple of weeks we were playing our first Hope gig, easy as you like. For me, this show of unquestioning inclusion of strangers was completely different from the response I was used to getting from people in Dublin. It took me by complete surprise and laid a precedent for everything musical that I've been involved in since.

During the following year or two, I met loads of people who were involved in the "cheap gig" music scene in Dublin. The bass player from **Jackbeast** ended up recording the only **Null Set** release. I started putting on shows under "Alpha Relish." I've been lucky enough to have played countless shows with countless bands, and made some amazing friends along the way.

Since then, I've put on a handful of shows, put out a couple of records, and tend to dance a lot on the weekend. I'm certain that without Hope, it wouldn't have occurred to me to do these things or I at least wouldn't have had the confidence to, especially the dancing on weekends . . . inspired by the Dillon family dancers, do do do de de dooooooooooooooooo.

It's such a joy to be able to work with the amazing people who are around Dublin at the moment, but it didn't get like this overnight." —*Hag, Null Set, Franci, O, Daemien Frost + Alpha Relish*

Jackbeast

ABHINANDA + STARMARKET + NECKWEED | FUSION, AUG. 24, 1997

VEGGIE LASAGNA

Ingredients

2 bell peppers

1 onion

a couple cloves of garlic (I'm a five a day man meself)

some mushrooms (if there has to be a number, four is as good as any)

1 carrot

some chickpeas (canned or frozen or dried as long as they're already cooked)

1 1/2 cups of veggie stock

1 small can tomato paste (you know what I'm talking about)

some assorted herbs

the old reliables—salt and pepper

some sheets of the lasagna pasta stuff

For the white sauce:

some marg, some flour, some soy milk, some oil for frying

Preparation

1. First off: To make your tomatoey sauce: Dice all your veggies and get a large saucepan. Now fry the veg: start with the onions and garlic and then add the peppers and carrot and so forth til all the veggies are added. Once things are lookin' good add your stock. Now add the tomato paste and herbs. Now let it simmer for, oh about half an hour, then add all those peas, chickpeas, corn and you're laughing. Now you're ready for the oven. But first: BEFORE you go to the oven you must make a sauce.

2. Well here it is. The sauce: Get some marg and melt in a small saucepan. Now add some flour a little at a time stirring constant like, (this took me ages to get used to so don't worry if you fuck up). Now you get what is referred to as a roux (a paste of flour and marg). Add some soy milk and stir til you get a thick saucy mixture. (Oh behave!) This is basically your common or garden white sauce recipe with soy milk instead of cow juice. If you like, add some nutritional yeast. This makes the sauce kinda cheesy (nice).

3. And finally to the oven: Right. You got to preheat this baby so hopefully you read this recipe fully before you started—if not, switch on the oven and sit yourself down. The oven has to be preheated to 450°F. Right: so now you should have one pot of tomatoey stuff and one pot of white sauce. So what you do is this: get your oven dish in which you are about to cook the lasagna and put lasagna sheets in the bottom, then put in some sauce, then some sheets. Right, depending on how big your dish is or how small your pot is you're going to get a certain number of layers, so what I like to do (if I have the time) is on top of one layer crumple up some tofu and on top of another lay some spinach. When you get to the last of the tomatoey sauce put on your sheets and pour over your white sauce. Now place it in the oven for a while (til it browns on top) and there you have it: animal-free lasagna.

"Some extras you might like to add: some corn (again don't care where you get them as long as they're cooked); some peas (ditto); a block of tofu (I recommend that you don't buy the stuff that comes in a carton 'cos in my experience it's muck, it's too watery and will disintegrate if you try to fry it, it does taste awful too. So only buy stuff if you can feel its texture is solid); some spinach; some nutritional yeast."
—Stephen, Neckweed + Tetsuo

HAL AL SHEDAD + CASTLES & CAR WRECKS + BAMBI FUSION, SEPT. 21, 1997

We had gotten some criticism for putting on the D.I.Y. Festival for the second year in the City Arts Centre. Deko organised a "Y.I.D. not D.I.Y." festival in his latest venue, the Old Chinaman.

There was a backlash against Hope and criticism started flying. We were even being written about in the toilets of venues.

I took the criticism personally and got annoyed over it. By now I had been involved in putting on gigs independently for thirteen years. The whole Hope thing was being mocked because some of the people in bands were students.

It was similar to left wing organizations bickering about who is the more valid revolutionary while the system remains intact. We weren't "punk enough" for the punks. Ironically, though, the Y.I.D. festival was organised at a different time from the D.I.Y. so that people could go down and see **Wat Tyler**.

Abhinanda and **Starmarket** were the first Swedish bands to visit Ireland through Hope and now **Hal Al Shedad** were over in Ireland from the U.S. We never asked if they were students or not. We never cared.

As for being Hope being "punk," no two people could ever give the same explanation so I can't really say if we were or were not.

HAL AL LASAGNA

Ingredients

1 box lasagna noodles
1 block firm tofu
1 package frozen shredded spinach
1 onion (chopped)
some nutritional yeast
some garlic
some pasta sauce of your liking
baking dish the length of your noodles, and 3 times their width
aluminum foil

Note: The important thing here is the tofu spinach that will replace that nasty cheese that your mama used. Once you prepare the tofu spinach magic, just follow the directions on your lasagna noodle box using the tofu spinach instead of cheese.

Preparation

1. Oil up a large pan or wok and turn the heat to high.
2. Add frozen spinach and onion into pan.
3. Crumble tofu into pan. Add the garlic.
4. Keep stirring and cooking on high until you feel all that stuff is cooked and most of the water from the tofu and spinach has cooked off.
5. Throw in some nutritional yeast flakes. Stir. Throw in some more if you like. Stir.
6. Now make your lasagna.

"And remember lasagna is always yummier the next day, reheated. Also it freezes well and you can then try adventurous things like fried lasagna."

——*The hal al lasagna is expressed through Benjamin Lukens (ben@ultivac.com)*

BLUETIP + KEROSENE 454 + JACKBEAST + HYLTON WEIR
FUSION, OCT. 26, 1997

Two bands from Washington, D.C., and both linked to Dischord records. It made for a great gig. **Hylton Weir** came down from Dundalk to play. Dundalk was playing host to many good gigs at this stage and it deservedly established a good reputation as a town for bands to visit.

Mir and I had moved home to Duleek,

twenty-five miles north of Dublin, so it was ideal for bands to stop by on their way down from Dundalk and Belfast.

The neighbors in the small village were all intrigued when they saw any visitors. The kids from down the road just wanted them to play soccer.

FAT FREE SALSA RISOTTO THING

Ingredients

big handful of tricolore farfalle (or any other pasta)

big handful of long-grain rice

1 head broccoli

1 1/2 cup vegan TVP chunks (or equivalent)

14 oz can chopped tomatoes

1 tbsp Religious Experience "Wrath of God" salsa (from USA)

2 cubes vegan vegetable stock

1/2 tsp garlic salt

1 tsp mixed herbs

Preparation

1. Put two saucepans of salted water on to boil. When boiling add the broccoli florets to one and the pasta to the other.

2. When the pasta is soft, bung in the rice and simmer til soft.

3. Drain both saucepans and bung everything back into the largest pan.

4. Bung in the vegan TVP chunks and the can of chopped tomatoes and stir.

5. Add the rest of the ingredients and simmer for 5 minutes.

6. Serve it and eat it.

7. Easy, ain't it?

"This is fat-free so if there are any overweight vegans out there who want to lose some weight (not like Wat Tyler!), this is for you. I made this up when I had run out of proper food so I found a load of things in cupboards and made it up as I went along. I made something else for the kids 'cos I knew it would be too hot for them. Nine times out of ten, making it up as you go along is a disaster, but this one worked out okay.

The "Wrath Of God" salsa sauce is the best in the world—you can use other salsa sauces if you can't get it, but get it if you can.

It takes about 10 minutes to make so it is also quick and easy."

—Smithy Wat Tyler

THE VAN PELT + 0 + SIN EATERS + BLACKBELT JONES
FUSION, NOV. 8, 1997

The licensing laws in Dublin meant that all gigs were due to end when the bars stopped serving beer. Generally this was at 11 P.M. I never objected to this as it meant that people had the option of taking the 11:30 last bus home.

We used to figure out times for bands on the night of the gig. The scientific method was to work backwards from the length of the last band's set and the number of groups appearing.

We only ever allowed 5–10 minutes between each band, so if things were to over-run it might take from the last band's time-frame. This rarely happened. If things were behind schedule it was taken from everyone's time. The only thing that couldn't be factored in was if a band took a long time to set up and that band was last on stage. This happened to **Van Pelt** tonight. They took an age to get going and then when they finally started they had to stop after a few songs.

The Van Pelt weren't happy after this one bit. They even spoke about it in a widely-distributed *Punk Planet* interview. It livened up one of our meetings afterwards. Lack of communication on the night meant that they were very unhappy with their time slot. They were still complaining when we gave them extra money on the evening.

TASTY MAMA'S PASTA

Ingredients

1 onion, finely chopped
pinch chili powder
1 tbsp mixed herbs
1 tbsp curry powder
1 jar tomato sauce
cooked pasta (as per pack instructions)
oil for frying

Preparation

1. Get a pot and put in a drop of sun-flower oil then wait for it to heat up.
2. Add the onion into the oil.
3. Add the chili powder, mixed herbs, and curry powder.
5. Stir well, adding some tomato sauce. You can use Ragu (brand name pasta sauce) or else make your own with tomato paste.
6. Add pasta that has already been cooked with salt and pepper.
7. Stir and serve with pita bread, garlic bread, or even on its own . . . mmm, delicious. I live off the stuff.

"Thinking about the Hope days brings back loads of memories for me . . . tasty memories . . . what a pun . . ."

—*Richie Egan, Blackbelt Jones + Redneck Manifesto*

CHEAPSKATE + RESIDENCE + NULL SET + WALTONS
FUSION, DEC. 12, 1997 | BENEFIT FOR RATHMINES WOMEN'S REFUGE

Christmas came around again and the Women's Refuge was still in operation. Again we charged £2 or a toy of equal value. Yet again sacks of toys were brought to Rathmines.

Paraic and James from **Cheapskate** were part of the Hope Collective. Paraic also ran a distro and accumulated a lot of stock. He used to set it up at the gigs. Table after table was laid out with fanzines, records, CDs, and tapes. It was great to see people coming along and buying stuff. That was their participation, but hopefully it didn't just end there.

Residence were from Wicklow and were influenced by American hardcore. They always attracted a good crowd whenever they played, but unfortunately most of the people only wanted to see them.

The Waltons were a hybrid mix of anything messed up. Their songs were full of noise with a little tune thrown in now and again to hold your interest.

The Null Set also had a hybrid sound but were not as noisy as the other bands on offer tonight.

One interesting point about this evening and a good indicator of the way the "scene" was heading: All the bands that played tonight have since released their own music. This is something that would not have happened a few years previously and may have a few factors involved: There is more disposable money around, and there is also more information about how to do things yourself. People have seen others do it and have followed suit.

TRACTOR PUNK CURRY

Ingredients

1 medium onion, diced
1 oz cashew nut
1/2 inch ginger, grated or finely chopped
2 chilis, finely chopped
3 cloves garlic, finely chopped
3 carrots, cut chunky
1 can of tomatoes
3 good-sized spuds, cut chunky
1 medium head of cauliflower, chopped
    handful of mushrooms
small zucchini
1/2 packet of creamed coconut
1 tbsp sugar
fresh cilantro, handful roughly chopped
1 can water
sunflower oil for frying
pinch of salt
1 tsp curry powder
1/2 tsp turmeric

Preparation

1. Sauté the onion, chilis, garlic, and ginger in hot oil with a handful of cashew nuts.
2. When cashews go brown, take off heat.
3. Now add the carrots, tomatoes (mushed up), water, salt, curry powder, turmeric, and a few raisins if ya like. Stir and bring to the boil.
4. When boiling add 3 spuds, cauliflower and mushrooms. When bubbling lower heat and add the zucchini.
5. Cook until spuds are nice and soft.
6. When cooked add creamed coconut, sugar, and cilantro.

—*Niall Byrne, Cheapskate*

CHEAPSKATE + STOMACH + DEBT
FUSION, JAN. 23, 1998 | BENEFIT FOR IRISH REFUGEE COUNCIL

EBULLITION SOUP

Ingredients

4 tbsp margarine
1 medium onion
1/4 lb sliced mushrooms
1 cup barley, pearled
2 cups broth
1/2 tsp salt

Preparation

1. Fry the onion, mushrooms, and barley in the margarine until the barley is brown (real brown).
2. Then put everything into a pan and add the broth and salt.
3. The pan should be fairly large so that the mixture isn't more than an inch to 1.5 inches deep. Bake it in the oven for around 1 hour at 350°F.

"Eat and enjoy."

—Kent McClard, Ebullition Records

PASTA AND CHICKPEAS

Ingredients + Preparation

1. Chop a clove of garlic as finely as you can and cook gently in olive oil.
2. Add a can of drained chickpeas (or soaked pre-cooked chickpeas if you can be bothered; I like canned better though) and stir til heated through.
3. Add to hot, cooked pasta (the shells are best as they "hold" the chickpeas!), stir well and eat! You can add chopped parsley if you like and vegan cheese if you eat it.

SECRET SAUCE

Ingredients + Preparation

1. Chop onions and garlic and cook in olive oil gently until transparent.
2. Add as many chopped veggies as you have/like. It is particularly good if you put in some red and yellow bell peppers that have been roasted for a while in the oven, but even when not roasted they add a nice flavor. I usually put in carrots, bell peppers, zucchinis, and maybe mushrooms. Also add 1 tsp oregano.
3. When the veggies are a little soft, add one or two cans of chopped tomatoes (or

ordinary canned toms), a small teaspoon of sugar, salt, pepper and a good dollop of tomato paste. If it seems really thick, add some stock or if it's for grownups who drink . . . a good slosh of red wine is nice. Cook all this until veggies are soft and sauce is thick and then whiz the hell out of it with a hand blender or allow to cool a bit and put in a big blender. This is good for pasta, pizzas, and so on.

"I make this for my kids and it is called this because they don't know that it is chock-full of veg!"

—Kirsten Bechoffer

KABINBOY + RESIDENCE + BLACKBELT JONES
FUSION, FEB. 13, 1998 | BENEFIT FOR ZAPATISTA ACTION PROJECT

Wat Tyler

Our meetings were still being held weekly, which was proving a bit of a strain for Mir and I. We lived 25 miles away and some nights we just wanted to go home after work.

When these meetings meant organizing a gig for a band that couldn't care less about being in Dublin and were willing to openly complain about our efforts, it was disheartening.

When the meetings consisted of arguments over what bands should play what gigs, it all got a bit much.

We tried to have consensus decisions on everything within the group, and with that in mind there were some long debates about various mind-numbing topics. It was important to be comfortable with everything the collective did, but things ended up taking more time than necessary.

One such discussion was about which organizations we would try to raise money for. Much like the square peg into a round hole analogy, there just wasn't enough time for all the groups we would have liked to help and many were put on the "must get around to" list.

Unfortunately, some of these were never dealt with. We did decide that we would only do benefit gigs if the bands were from outside Dublin, something I never argued about.

ROCK CAKES

Ingredients

- 2 cups self-rising flour (or 2 cups all-purpose flour and 4 tsp baking powder)
- 1 pinch salt
- a couple drops of flavoring essence (too much and you'll know about it)
- 1/3 cup margarine
- 1/3 cup sugar (soft cane or "pieces" sugar)
- about 1/2 cup soy milk or water

Preparation

1. Sift the flour and salt. Rub in margarine and add sugar.
2. Mix with the liquid and add essence (not too much, it'll kill ya) to a dropping consistency. (At this stage it is sometimes nice to throw in something interesting like raisins or whatever ya like.)
3. Place mixture in spoonfuls on greased baking sheet, or in patty cans, or my favorite— cupcake holders, and bake in hot oven (450°F) for 10 to 15 minutes. Makes about 12 buns.

—*Anna, Kabinboy*

MASAMBA, JOAN OF ARSE, FRANCI FUSION, FEB. 27, 1998 | BENEFIT FOR GENETIC CONCERN

After **Bloco Vomit** played the previous summer, we were keen on getting another Samba band to play a gig.

MaSamba was a samba band based in the City Arts Centre and were receptive to the idea. They were more used to playing larger free festivals and protests so the intimate setting of the Fusion Bar was probably not too appealing. You'd never guess, though, as they took to the stage and the dance floor and got everyone moving.

SPINACH AND GINGER BOWEL LOOSENER

Ingredients

good heap of spinach, chopped small
1 clove garlic, finely chopped
4 mushrooms
olives
1/4 lb tofu, diced
lemon juice
vegetable stock cube
2 onions, finely chopped
1 tsp ground ginger
black pepper to taste
soy sauce
olive oil for frying

Preparation

1. Boil spinach in plenty of water. Adding a stock cube to the water is a good idea: it makes the spinach tastier, plus you can use the now vitamin-filled stock (thanks to the spinach) as the basis of a soup.

2. Marinate your tofu whatever way you want, but for consistency, you could do it in some of the veg stock and add a bit of soy sauce for color.

3. To add texture to the dish, after the tofu is good and flavor soaked, you could grill on a medium temperature til it starts to brown and then add it in to the mix towards the end. It makes it a bit crunchy.

4. Next, fry the onions in the olive oil, let them get a head start and then add the chopped garlic, mushrooms, and sprinkle with some ginger and black pepper.

5. As they get nearer to being done, strain the spinach (but don't throw out that lovely stock!!) and sprinkle heavily with ginger.

6. Add the olives and lemon juice and mix around making sure you get plenty of ginger and lemon throughout.

"When it's all good and mixed, lay it out in a bowl and add the onion/mushroom/garlic and tofu and serve on pasta or rice, or with potatoes. If you have some left over, it's really nice on toast. Sin é."

—*The Bearded Lady, Joan of Arse + Shred + Groundswell + Not Our World*

VANILLA POD + ONE CAR PILE UP + DISSENT
FUSION, MARCH 13, 1998

VEGETABLE CASSEROLE

Ingredients

2 onions, sliced
3 cloves garlic, crushed
1/2 cup carrots, sliced
1 large potato, peeled and cubed
10 closed cup mushrooms, sliced
4 oz frozen peas
2 tbsp paprika
1 can baked beans
2 cups vegetable stock
2 tbsp tomato paste
1 large glass of red wine or cider

Preparation

1. Sauté the onion, garlic, carrots, potato, peas, mushrooms, and paprika in a little olive oil for 5 mins.
2. Add beans, tomato paste, and the vegetable stock.
3. Bring to the boil and simmer for 30 min.
4. Serve with baked potatoes or dumplings made with vegetable suet.

"This can be used with any variation of different vegetables if you don't like any of the above."

—*Steve Pod*

WINTER VEGETABLE SOUP

Ingredients

3 onions, chopped coarsely
2 veggie stock cubes (or fresh vegetable stock if you have it)
3 potatoes, cut into large chunks
2 carrots, cut into large chunks
2 parsnips, cut into large chunks
1/2 small pumpkin, cut into large chunks
3 sticks of celery, large chunks
1 mug soup mix (barley, lentil, etc.)
water
6 cloves of garlic, chopped finely
assorted herbs + spices: salt, pepper, rosemary, parsley, thyme, oregano, bay leaves, etc., to taste
oil for frying

Preparation

1. Brown the onions in a little oil.
2. Add water: 4 or 8 cups to begin with and you can add more later as you require.
3. Add the soup mix, chopped vegetables, garlic, herbs, and spices.
3. Bring to boil and simmer for 1 to 2 hours.
4. The pumpkin will disintegrate, thickening the soup. If you find the soup too thick, just add more water. Serve piping hot!

"This vegetable soup is perfect for those cold winter nights. The ingredients above are for a very large quantity—this recipe freezes well, so what you don't use you can freeze. You will need the biggest pot you have, or else you can reduce the ingredients appropriately. The spices and herbs listed are just my preferences—you can add cumin or paprika or whatever else takes your fancy."

—*Brian Bannon Ogre, Pans Apprentice*

CONSUME + CONSCIOUS + RESIDENCE
FUSION, APRIL 26, 1998

TAHINI BANANA TOAST

Ingredients + Preparation

1. Toast a piece of whole-grain bread. Spread on a layer of sesame tahini.
2. Cut a banana in half lengthwise and put on top. Great for breakfast!

"Tahini is a paste made only from sesame seeds. It comes in a variety of thickness and bitterness. I find the canned Joya brand to be bitter and not so great. Arrowhead Mills and Woodstock both make tahini in jars which is very good."

MAPLE SWEET POTATO PUDDING

Ingredients + Preparation

1. Peel 6 or so large sweet potatoes (or yams). Cut into 1-inch cubes.
2. Lightly oil the inside of a ceramic or metal pot that has a tight lid and can go into the oven.
3. Add chopped sweet potatoes.
4. Add about 1 1/2 cups of pure maple syrup.
5. Add 1/4 tsp salt, 1/2 tsp nutmeg, 1/4 tsp cinnamon.
6. Add 3 tbsp water (or enough so that the water/syrup covers at least 3/4 of the sweet potatoes).
7. Mix all together. Bake in 350°F oven for an hour. Stir once after 1/2 hour. When it is done, let cool a bit, then mash completely.

"Sweet dessert! Good hot or chilled."
—Arik Grier, Fat Day

LEMON NO PELICAN SOUP

Ingredients

3 cups vegetable stock
1 cup dry cider
1/2 cup short-grain brown rice
salt and pepper
2 lemons, juiced, rind grated
2 tbsp chives, snipped
4 thin lemon slices to garnish

Preparation

1. Simmer the stock, cider, and rice in a covered pot with salt, pepper, and lemon rind for 40 minutes.
2. Purée and return to the pot. Mix in the lemon juice & simmer gently.
3. Cool and skim any fat that might appear on the surface. Chill.
4. To serve, scatter with the chives and garnish each bowl with a slice of lemon.
5. Add as much cider as you would deem necessary.

"Serves four people, i.e., the band."
—Brendan Butler, LMNO Pelican

REFUSED + INK & DAGGER + HYLTON WEIR
MCGRATHS, MAY 23, 1998

Fusion didn't want to put uneccessary attention on their business by having a gig in the afternoon, so we had to look elsewhere. We wanted this to be an afternoon gig with no age restirictions.

Doug (owner of Fusion) ran a club in McGraths so we asked if **Refused**, from Sweden, **Ink & Dagger** from Philadelphia, USA, and **Hylton Weir** from Dundalk could all play there on the afternoon at his club (also called Fusion).

He persuaded McGrath's management to go with it. It was then possible for the bands to troop up to Dundalk for another gig that evening.

Refused came with a reputation of being political but musically they were a little bit different. They impressed most of the crowd present.

The venue was on the third floor of McGraths. There was no elevator and there was no parking out front. We hauled up the fire escape with all the equipment. It was a nightmare. Luckily, it wasn't a wet day, as the stairs would have been hazardous. As things stood it was very hard on the back and we realized exactly how heavy some musical equipment can be.

Refused

ABHINANDA, RESIDENCE, LOW END FUSION, SEPT. 4, 1998

This was **Abhinanda**'s second trip to Ireland to play some shows. They played Cork, Dundalk, Dublin and Belfast to an average of 100 people in each place. They opened up many people's eyes to the extistence of music in Europe. For many Irish people their musical interests end west of Britain and east of America (take out your atlas to find out where that is).

Residence sent us a demo tape and any time I think about the liner note, "This goes out to all the homies in Superquinn Bray," I chuckle. I wonder if they do too.

BEANS AND CHIPS

Ingredients + Preparation

1. Take £1.50 from the communal money.
2. Get a saucepan and can opener ready.
3. Go to the shop and buy a can of Heinz (or other brand) baked beans and a cheap shitty white loaf of sliced bread.
4. Go to the chip shop and get a portion of chips wrapped up to make sure they don't lose too much heat while heating the beans.
5. Open the beans and heat them as quickly as you can. Stir occasionally whilst getting the chips on the plate.
6. Pick at the chips while waiting for the beans.
7. Add the beans to the chips.
8. Make two or three sandwiches with beans and chips.
9. Finish everything else off.
10. Leave the washing up to someone else.

—*Sean, Wat Tyler*

PUNKGRYTA (PUNK CASSEROLE)

Ingredients

1 cup rice
1 onion, diced
3 cloves garlic, minced
1/2 tsp paprika
pinch saffron threads (optional, often in +300 venues)
15 oz can chickpeas
2 cups chopped tomatoes
spices (whatever you might find)
1 or 2 other vegetables of free choice

Preparation

1. Overcook rice in 2 cups of water.
2. Sauté onion, garlic, paprika, other vegetables, spices and saffron (if desired). Cook over medium high heat, stirring frequently until onions are soft. This takes about about 8 minutes.
3. Add chickpeas, 1/2 cup of their liquid and tomatoes. Lower heat and simmer for 15 minutes. If pan becomes dry, add a little water to keep it moist.
4. Put rice in casserole, add chickpea-tomato mixture.
5. Toss until well mixed.

"This is what a touring band don't want to get when they arrive hungry after driving 8 hours, but always get (at least 90 percent of the shows) . . . and learns to appreciate while 'on the road' and actually finds tasty . . . A phenomenon called Punkgryta in Sweden . . ."

—*Jose, Abhinanda*

POLARIS + NULL SET + HYLTON WEIR | FUNNEL, OCT. 26, 1998

The Attic had now closed down and Barnstormers was gone, as was Charlie's. Fusion had been the Hope Collective's regular venue but that was proving harder to get.

Another new venue started up beside the City Arts Centre called the Funnel. It was really nice—a two-level bar complete with PA. It was customised for live music, and although it was more expensive than Fusion, it was worth it. We were looking forward to using it a lot more after tonight's gig.

BOLOGNESE

Ingredients

2 onions
I clove garlic
3 carrots
I red bell pepper
I small zucchini
2 cans of tomatoes
some mushrooms
celery or other such veg as you please, leeks go well
I can of cider/lager
2 cups of unflavoured TVP (soy protein) bits, oregano, fresh if possible, thyme, and whatever YOU like
mustard
olive paté (if you have some anyway)
tomato paste

Preparation

1. Soak the TVP in the cider. Do this either the night before you cook or anytime up to when you start—the longer you leave it to soak the more absorbent of other flavors it becomes.

2. Chunky-chop the onions and fry slowly in an unstingy amount of oil. Let them go transparent, rather than brown.

3. Dice the carrots, pepper, zucchini, and other veggies and add to the onions, following the basic principle of the crunchiest going in first.

4. Cook to the point that they are shiny and colorful, then add the garlic, herbs, and mustard, salt and pepper.

5. Give a good stir about and then add the TVP/cider mix. Leave simmering on a lowish heat so all the flavors merge.

6. After 5 or 10 minutes, depending on how hungry you are or how much time you have, add the tomatoes.

7. Again, leave to simmer for as long as possible—up to around 45 minutes.

"This recipe is one way of giving TVP a taste other than that of rehydrated rabbit droppings."
—Hag, Null Set, Franci, O, Daemien Frost, Alpha Relish

DROP DEAD + JOHN HOLMES | CLODAGHS FLAT, NOV. 26, 1998

TOFU PIE THINGY

Okay—this is a recipe that is extremely versatile in that you can just cook whatever you want and either throw it in a prebought pie shell or little pie shells; cover it or don't cover it; or use it as a bake with pasta shells; or anything that you can think of. I've even used it as the bottom of a shepard's pie and topped it with mashed potatoes.

Tofu

Take FIRM tofu and squeeze the excess water out. Cut into one-inch cubes. On a plate mix equal parts of flour and nutritional yeast flakes and stir. Roll the cubes in the powder, evenly coating them. Then fry them all up, being careful not to stir, but to turn, so that they don't break up. You should end up with a batch of golden brown cubes of tofu with extra added flavor from the yeast flakes.

Veggies

I usually fry up the essential onion, with whatever else I have at home or is on sale at the shops. Broccoli, carrots, peas, and all that stuff should be cut up fine and boiled until just tender. Other veggies like mushrooms, peppers, and spinach should be fried up with the onion. Throw in some garlic too. I always add a can or two of corn, 'cos it rules.

Golden Gravy (this is the good thing)

1/4 cup flour
1/2 cup nurutional yeast
1/3 cup margarine
1 1/2 cup water

2–3 tbsp soy sauce or tamari
salt and pepper

Toast the flour and the nutritional yeast flakes until they give off a nutty aroma. Add oil or margarine and stir until bubbly. Add water and cook until the mixture begins to thicken, stirring constantly. I usually use a whisk for this part. Add soy sauce and salt and pepper. Makes approximately two cups. So then everything is all mixed together—being careful not to break up the tofu.

Then you have the perfect filling for a killer pie . . . or the perfect thing to mix with a buttload of pasta twirls to then throw back in the oven and bake for a while.

—*Vique Martin, Simba fanzine*

GARLIC BEANS ON TOAST

Ingredients + Preparation

1. Chop up a load of garlic and throw into a can of beans.
2. Get the margarine you'd usually put on the toast and throw that in the bean/garlic mix.
3. Some kinda chemical reaction occurs and it makes it all goo up a lot better. Then spread it on the toast.

—*Sned, John Holmes*

THE SORTS + THE REDNECK MANIFESTO | FUNNEL, DEC. 6, 1998

The first time **The Redneck Manifesto** played in Dublin there were huge expectations. Featuring ex-members of **Hylton Weir**, **Blackbelt Jones**, **The Waltons** and **Flexihead**, it was our hardcore "supergroup."

They surprised many and let down very few. Their sound was unlike any of their previous bands. There were no vocals but their intense stage presence captivated listeners.

Since their first gig a lot has been said in Dublin about their independent stance and the fact that the band try to exercise control over everything they do.

Knowing that all four members used to go to Hope gigs, it makes me proud to see them. They are not leading the way—just doing what they want to, when they want to and I salute them for it.

1998 ended for the Hope Collective with this gig. It was a relatively quiet year, with only 11 gigs—not even one a month.

Mir and I were losing interest and the meetings were becoming more sporadic. Miriam was now expecting our first child and this was a lot more exciting than the thoughts of a touring band playing. Hope never existed just to be a factory for touring bands and sometimes it felt like we had become that—Dublin one day, anywhere else the next. To me that was never the point.

COLCANNON (KALE)

Ingredients

4–5 good size potatoes
some soy milk or margarine
cooked colcannon (also know as kale), chopped
onions chopped (not too finely)
sea salt and fresh ground black pepper to taste

Preparation

1. Cook and mash the potatoes with the milk or margarine 'til you get the consistency you want.
2. Add as much colcannon and onions as fits your taste.
3. Season with salt and pepper. (Someone said to add nutmeg but I've never tried this.)
4. You can have this with some kind of veggie/vegan sausage and beans.

—*Niall Byrne, Redneck Manifesto*

The Farewell Band

BLUETIP + FAREWELL BEND + THE REDNECK MANIFESTO
FUNNEL, MARCH 26, 1999

Bluetip's second Dublin appearance was in the excellent Funnel. We hadn't used the venue often and it stopped doing gigs soon after.

The owner sold the bar license on elsewhere and therefore it closed down. It would have been nice for it to continue solely as a venue but that wouldn't have paid the bills. It would have been great, though.

Bluetip were travelling with fellow Americans **Farewell Bend**, and **The Redneck Manifesto** topped off a very entertaining evening.

LOS VAQUEROS DE LA CALLE VEGAN BURRITOS (MEXICAN STYLE)

Ingredients

2 tsp olive oil
14 oz package of tofu, diced
4 broccoli crowns, chopped
2 mushrooms, chopped
2 large garlic cloves, thinly chopped
1/4 of a red bell pepper, chopped
1/8 cup onions, chopped
1 tomato, diced
1 avocado, sliced
1/8 cup lettuce or spinach, chopped
1 can chopped olives
2 servings cooked rice
2 large flour tortillas (Mexican style—made with no lard)

Preparation

1. Prepare all of the vegetables while you are cooking the rice (as per pack's instructions) You can use any kind of rice you prefer.
2. Put olive oil into a large skillet, set burner to medium high and begin heating. Once hot, dump in the goods: 7oz of tofu, broccoli crowns, mushrooms, garlic, bell pepper and onions.
3. Put the rest of the vegetables on a plate and set aside.
4. Sauté vegetables until slightly brown. They should be steaming. Be sure to stir so that nothing burns to your nice skillet.
5. Once done you can heat up the tortillas in the oven or on a burner. Make sure it's evenly heated. This is a very important step. If the tortilla isn't properly heated it will crack while you're attempting to eat it causing the ingredients to spill from the burrito violently. So be careful.
6. Place one tortilla on each plate. Pour half of the sauteed vegetable and tofu mix onto each tortilla spread out in the middle so that you'll be able to roll it.
7. Each person then adds his or her own toppings from the uncooked vegetables.
8. Be sure to put about three spoonfuls of rice on each burrito.
9. Fill it up with all the goodies.
10. It's a little hard to explain the rolling process so just experiment. I fold one side of the tortilla over and then roll so that the top of the burrito is open and the bottom is closed.

"Find a nice spot to sit down and put on a good movie with a nice glass of wine or beer. Oooohhhh! Enjoy!"
—Terrin Durfey, Farewell Bend

MONTH OF BIRTHDAYS + CAPSTAN + JOAN OF ARSE + ESTEL
FUNNEL, APRIL 17, 1999

Four months into 1999 and we had the second Hope Collective gig. Mir and I rarely went to meetings. Tired of the traveling, we were concentrating a lot more on the impending birth.

Derek had gone to live in France and his departure had taken away a lot of the impetus. The meetings were still held in what had been Derek's place. Aoife and later Finbar also lived there but it always felt like Derek's place.

When he left there was no one really interested in holding it all together. Clodagh, Jamie and Anto were still keen but it became a struggle. Pete was concentrating on his web site, Thumped, and others were accusing us of not being punk enough.

Month Of Birthdays asked if they could play again and we were quite happy to accommodate them but that's all we were doing at that stage. It was still a good gig, though.

VEGAN SATAY

Ingredients

1 carrot
1/2 zucchini
1/2 head broccoli
8–10 average sized mushrooms
2 tbsp of peanut butter
nice big slab of tofu (frozen and defrosted gives a firmer texture)
some chili powder (as spicy as you like)
soy milk
soy sauce
lemon juice
balsamic vinegar (optional)
2 cloves of garlic
ginger
vegetable oil (tastes nicer if mixed with a bit of sesame seed oil)

Tofu

1. Chop the tofu into cubes.
2. Heat some oil in a pan at high heat.
3. Fry the tofu until it becomes slightly brown.
4. Carefully add some soy sauce and balsamic vinegar to give it a bit of flavour. Fry until dark brown. Put it onto a dish.

Veg

1. Chop your veg into sticks. Heat some more oil in your pan. Fry the veg on a high heat.
2. Add chopped garlic and ginger at the same time. Don't fry for long or it will go soggy.

Sauce

If you're lazy on the washing up like me you can make the sauce in the same pan as the veg.

1. Make a well in the middle of the veg. Add loads of soy sauce, loads of lemon juice, peanut butter, chili powder and gradually mix in soy milk until you get a nice creamy sauce.
2. Add more soy sauce or lemon juice to get a really full-on taste.
3. Add the tofu and mix it all up. If you are feeling extra plush, add some peanuts or cashew nuts.

Serve with rice or noodles (or both).

—*Cath O'Connor, Month Of Birthdays*

HAPPY ANGER + NULL SET + SIR KILLALOT FUSION, MAY 28, 1999

Derek had settled down in Lyon and befriended the band **Happy Anger**. They contacted us about doing some gigs. They were to be the last band that I would have dealings with.

Miriam was nearly due. **Happy Anger** were a really nice bunch of people but Fusion was full of smoke and no seats and Mir just wanted to get home. I was glad of the excuse and we left early with Mir feeling some pains. It was a quiet exit.

As we drove away from the Fusion Bar neither of us thought that this was to be our last real involvement in a Hope gig.

We weren't to think about it again for quite a while as Ellen's birth five days later consumed our lives. However, 15 years after **Vicarious Living** played in Tommy Dunnes there was approximately the same amount of people in Fusion to see **Happy Anger**.

This was the last Hope gig in the Fusion Bar, which closed soon after. The Hope Collective continued for another while but from now on I was on paternity leave.

The excitement that was to follow for us after Ellen was born has made for a new chapter in our lives. Another child (Robert) has since been born and I've been working on the completion of this book for the past three years, watching a child develop and seeing her perception of the world—a world we all help shape.

BEEF STEW

Ingredients

1 tube "gimme lean" (mock beef) or 1 cup TVP chunks (or Sosmix)
7/8 cup of boiling water
1 tsp lemon juice
1 onion, chopped
1 clove garlic, minced
1 tbsp oil
4 cups water
14 oz can tomatoes
1 tsp veggie worcestershire sauce
2 small bay leaves
2 tbsp salt
1/2 tsp pepper
1 pinch ground allspice
1 vegetable stock cube
1/4 tbsp sugar
6 carrots, chopped
3 potatoes cut to bite size
10 oz packet frozen peas
2 tbsp cornstarch dissolved in water

Preparation

1. Brown the onion and garlic in the oil, add the "beef" and continue browning.
2. Add the water, tomatoes, worcestershire sauce, bay leaves, salt, pepper, allspice, stock cube and sugar.
3. Simmer for 1 hour. Add the carrots, peas and potatoes.
4. Cook for another 30 minutes. Thicken with the cornstarch.

—*Liam, Sir Killalot + Underfoot*

ASTREAM + DROPNOSE + SIRKILLALOT | SLATTERY'S, JULY 13, 1999

PIZZA AL SYNDICALISTO

Ingredients

water
flour
yeast
salt
olive oil
I finely chopped onion
any Steve Earle album and a CD player
2 cloves chopped garlic
3 tbsp tomato paste
I can (14 oz) chopped tomatoes
drink of whiskey (or any alcoholic beverage)
I lb fresh spinach or 8 oz frozen fresh
basil
32 black olives, pitted
black pepper
sugar
a few Pfeferonies are always nice

Preparation

Pizza crust (look somewhere else, why not a cookbook, for correct measurement, cause I can't be arsed reverting from metric to "imperial"). Mix yeast with the flour. Add salt, oil and water. Cover and leave to rise for some time. (Again, see cookbook).

(Far be it from me to interrupt another person's recipe but there are clear instructions on packets of easy bake yeast on how to prepare dough. Don't get caught up in measurements and words like metric and imperial. After all they are only measurements. —Ed.)

Put on a Steve Earle CD and get cracking with the tomato sauce.

This was another new venue for Hope. The Funnel had closed its doors and Smiley Bolger (who had helped us out with the New Inn) was now looking after Slattery's so we held this gig there. Slattery's didn't last much longer as a venue. The curse of Hope?

TOMATO SAUCE

1. Fry the onion and the garlic in oil.
2. Add tomato paste and fry for a tad bit more.
3. Lower heat and add the tomatoes and a pinch of sugar.
4. Heat the oven to 475°F. Pour a drink for yourself and let the sauce cook on medium-low heat for as long as possible, but at least 25 minute.
5. By the end of cooking the sauce, when there's about 5 minutes left, you add the basil and salt & pepper.
6. Sort the spinach out. By now the base should be ready.
7. Grease up an oven tray, try to make a nice round shaped pizza for 2 hours, or just fuck it off and do a square one. Either will suffice.
8. Put the spinach on first, then the tomato sauce covering the whole base.
9. Randomly place the olives on top. (I reckon some grated tofu on top of it would be nice.)
10. Chuck it in the oven. Wait for approx. 20—25 minutes.
11. Serve with pfeferonies or vegan coleslaw. Eat.

—Robert Johnson, Astream

ESTEL + MILGRAM + REDNECK MANIFESTO | ISAAC BUTTS, NOV. 6, 1999

VEG CURRY

Ingredients

1 potato
1 carrot
1 onion
1 large head broccoli
1 can tomato (Shamrock herbs and spices)
2 handfuls TVP
2 tbsp curry paste (Shamrock's korma paste)
1/2 cup water

Preparation

1. Chop and boil veg until tender.
2. Finely chop onion and fry in 1 tbsp of the curry paste.
3. Add tomatoes, veg, and the rest of curry paste.
4. Add water and TVP.
5. Simmer for half-hour and serve with rice.

CHICKPEA CURRY

Ingredients

1 onion
1 can tomatoes
2 carrots
1 can chickpeas
2 tbsp curry paste
1/2 cup water

Preparation

1. Chop and boil carrots until tender.
2. Fry onion in 1 tbsp of the curry paste
3. Add tomatoes, chickpeas, carrots and water.
4. Simmer for 15–20 minutes; serve with rice or boiled potatoes.

—Sara, Estel

A new venue, Isaac Butts, had just opened. It seemed like a good place but was really expensive to hire. **Milgram** came over on the recommendation of their compatriots **Happy Anger**.

Hope had finished for me at this stage. I was more interested in Ellen and anything she had to do than in any band looking to play Ireland. I was starting to feel that bands no longer cared about where they were playing. Ireland was just another country, Dublin just another city.

The buzz from getting a band to play in this country was gone; the feeling of empowerment was no longer there. The sense of "we can do anything we want as long as we want to and work towards it" was still there deep down in my gut. It just took a bit of looking for and the possibility didn't excite me.

Having a baby excited me. The thoughts of following her progress through life excites (and scares) me. I didn't plan to stop my involvement in gigs; it just petered out that way.

So I missed **Milgram**, I missed **Estel**, and I missed **The Redneck Manifesto**. Ironically, given that many local bands used to be so short-lived, the Irish bands have outlasted that day's visitors and have gone on to record and self-release their own material, which is pleasing to see (and to listen to). This is a situation that probably would not have occurred in 1987 when Hope was first put on a poster. In its own small way, the existence of Hope has helped it to happen.

BLUETIP + BAMBI | ISAAC BUTTS, NOV. 13, 1999

Bambi had had this date booked well in advance as they were launching their latest record. **Bluetip** were looking to come back to Ireland for a third time and were in Dublin the same day.

Due to a lack of venues, and considering the fact that it would be crazy to have two gigs on the same day, we asked if **Bluetip** could gatecrash the **Bambi** party. **Bambi** said no problem and the gig went ahead.

HUSSIVE MIX CHILI BEAN

Ingredients

I large onion, chopped (not too small)
I can chili beans
I can baked beans
2 tbsp each ketchup, steak sauce, chili sauce
2 tbsp cajun powder (you can buy these in sachets)
I tbsp chili powder/Tabasco sauce
salt and pepper
a few spuds or rice (I prefer mashed spuds, cuz i'm a mucker)
oil for frying

Preparation

Right, friends, we all know how important the carbohydrates are, so here's a fiendishly tasty way to get them!! First of all, put on a Shellac or a Fall album—good cooking music and something you can sing along to.

1. The rice or spuds will take the longest, so put them on to boil first. Sit around for about 15 minutes, or do something you've been meaning to do for ages, like wash.
2. Now check the spuds/rice to see if they're on the way. If so, take out your pan. If you're really slick, you'll take out a Wok—but a deep sized pan will do.
3. Turn up the heat to nearly full. Add some oil, just enough to cover the bottom of the pan. Fry the onion.
4. Add some salt and pepper, about I tbsp of each. Now you'll get this massive smell that will make your squat or penthouse smell like the heavens.
5. Wait till the onions soften up, turn down the heat a tad and then add the two cans of beans.
6. Stir well, then add the ketchup and brown sauce—this will give it its main flavour.
7. Add the chili sauce with the cajun powder and chili powder (or Tabasco sauce). Stir well and wait for it to bubble a bit, but make sure it doesn't start sticking to the pan, cuz that'll be a pain in the arse to clean.
8. By now your spuds/rice will be ready. Put the heat down to a minimum on the beans and drain the spuds/rice (mash the spuds). Put the spuds/rice onto a plate and lash the beans on top. Turn up the stereo, grab the chilled flagon out of the fridge, sit down and enjoy.

"Note: if you peeled the spuds, keep the skins. They taste massive if you fry them in a pan and then dip them into hummus, ketchup . . . whatever."

—Willie, 21st century coffee shop boy, Bambi

THE SORTS + JOAN OF ARSE | JJ SMYTHS, DEC. 7, 1999

RED STUFF

Ingredients + Preparation

beans
red stuff, i.e., red sauce
add rice pasta or hair
cook and mix till smelly
then add bread and butter and pint of white
  blood
sit down and watch porn

—*Mero, Norvics, Dr Shitface*

TOFU TOASTIE

Ingredients

3 large mushrooms, chopped
2 cloves garlic
2 tbsp grated ginger
4 oz smoked tofu, diced
bread for sandwiches
oil for frying

Preparation

1. Fry mushrooms in oil with garlic and
   grated ginger.
2. Add tofu to the mix.
3. Put mixture between 2 slices of bread and
   put into sandwich toaster.
4. Eat.

—*Joss Moorkens, Capratone, Tucker Suite + Joan Of Arse*

This gig is now known retrospectively as the last Hope gig. I stopped going to meetings and told the people now in the Collective—Pete, Clodagh, Damien and Stephen—that I was no longer keen to be involved. I offered them assistance if they wanted it and should they wish to continue but I was no longer eager to traipse around town putting up posters. There were plenty of bands in Dublin and other people were doing gigs by independent bands.

Hope evolved out of a neccessity for someone to start doing stuff. That need was no longer there. However Hope itself evolved into the idea that people can be creative without waiting around for others to show them how. People can do things if they put their mind to it. If people have questions then they have answers to find out. If they don't like the answers they hear they can try and do something about it.

Simply put: If you've got something to complain about, you've got something to change.

Hope finished as a name on a poster in a venue that I had booked for the first (and only) time 12 years previously. The posters of Garret Fitzgerald (Taoiseach of the time) that we hung upside down on the wall behind us (with black masking tape over his mouth) are still around somewhere. In those intervening 12 years many, many friendships were created and some marvellous people came to gigs in Dublin. I am lucky to have been part of it.

HOPE—THE LEGACY

"Some beautiful moments, some blurred memories: Hanging onto a speaker, looking at Niall doing the same while the whole stage is being bounced up and down by a hundred girls who took over the front of the **Bikini Kill** gig. A crystal summer's morning on the front step of the house listening to the singer from Lungfish rasp out his "conspiracy facts." **Alice Donut** re-enacting the American presidential election in the kitchen.

Frankie Stubbs in an almost empty flat playing the best set I've ever heard. **Wat Tyler** miming a hurling match on a festival afternoon to a crowd crippled with laughter. Father Ted with **Ebola, Los Crudos** and **Sned**. Neil Turpin, Rob and 411 more times than I can remember. Coming home at 5 in the morning and having breakfast with **Brawl**. Screwball Scramble with **The Kabinboy**.

I don't know if you can measure the success of something like Hope. It wasn't something to be thought about in terms of success or failure. It was about thinking, doing, saying and making. It was about positive and negative, about having the widest effect possible, not just putting on bands and having people come and consume (although it was just that at times). It was a big bag of successes and failures all mixed in together.

For me the successes were the group of gigs we did around Christmas '96. At one, we asked everyone to bring canned food which was later given to a local organization that worked an outreach for homeless people. Toys were brought to a second which were later given to a local women's refuge—imagine, a gig where money doesn't come into it, no money changes hands, everyone participates, everyone is a participant and the result is the astonished look on the refuge manager's face when we arrived with bag after bag of toys.

Success was also the festival we put together with Alison from the City Arts Centre—gigs, food, workshops, roundtables and a bunch of collectives from all kinds of backgrounds with a mixture of people of all ages—a really impressive experience.

Failure was the benefit we put on for the people of Chiapas, Mexico with **The Kabinboy** from Belfast, where nobody wanted to listen. They just wanted to "rock"; obviously we didn't do the best job of explaining the reasons for the gig. At the time, massacres in Chiapas were regular occurrences.

Failure was maybe also not paying attention to the changing situation in the "DIY music industry" that had begun around the same time as the Collective. Sometimes I wonder if we didn't help the "real" promoters take over. I wonder if we could have done something differently to perpetuate the ideas that we had, especially the lack of importance that money played. I don't know if Hope was something that could have or should have lasted. The biggest contradiction was simply the fact that the more popular the music became, the less place there was for the politics and the more attractive the whole thing became for people whose prime motivation was money.

Hope's legacy is not something immediately visible to my mind. I think anyone who has organised, played at or seen a Hope gig has that experience as part of them; I'm sure it affects us all to a larger or smaller degree in what we do and how we do it. Hope—before, during and after my involvement—helped form me. The ideas that were fundamental then still are. Don't like something? Change it. Missing something? Create it.

Hope, **Fugazi**, *React*, *Gearhead Nation*, Radioactive all came from the same place—they're all part of the same thing and they're all part of me. Without them I wouldn't have had the immense honour of meeting all of the people involved—collective members, bands and audience. So thank you everyone who helped, played and supported. And to Niall and Miriam, thank you for creating something that I'll always be proud to have been a part of. I can't remember exactly when it was, '97 or '98, that Anto Dillon approached me about joining the ranks of the Hope Collective. Shortly afterwards, one evening myself and my friend Jamie Farrell went to a Hope meeting.

I remember we used to get together weekly in the flat of Derek and Finbarr, where Miriam and Niall, Jamie and I, Anto and Eugene, Pete, James, Aoife and one or two others at different times sat around, drank tea, ate biscuits, had a laugh, oh! and organised gigs for Irish and touring bands.

I'm not sure why exactly I was asked to join; perhaps they were under the illusion that it was new blood and there would be some youthful enthusiasm. I didn't have much of that. It appeared to me that the Hope Collective had it all sewn up—the venues, the flyer and poster design and distribution, the actual running of the gig on the night.

In those days, I'm sorry to say I didn't pull my weight as much as I could have. Everything was sorted by the older, more experienced, together people. They made it look easy (as anyone who is good at what they do can). I felt it was more enjoyable to get pissed at a gig rather than help out at it.

Between then and now lots of things have changed—people have become less involved, some moved away, venues have closed. The Celtic Tiger came about. There was marriage, there are kids, there are mortgages. Pete "was" Hope and ran the scene single-handedly (or seemed to) for a while, The Kids appeared and continued doing things in the way the Hope Collective inspired us to.

These days I'm still actively involved in putting on gigs, formerly with The Kids and now in Groundzero Club in The Parnell Mooney on Thursday nights. The scene is vibrant. I am the same age now as those "mature," "experienced" people were back in the Hope Collective days of the Blessington Street flat.

These days there is at least one underground/DIY/independent gig on somewhere in the city most nights. Sometimes there is too much to choose from.

Although I failed to engage with what was going on as much as I might have in the early days I am very glad for having had the opportunity to observe the Hope Collective at work. If they hadn't taken me under their wing all those years ago, I would never have had the confidence to do what I do now. They built the foundation for a healthy underground music scene in Dublin, and I endeavor to continue this tradition.

I have spoken to other people involved in other parts of Ireland who mention Hope gigs as being influential in their involvement in creating a DIY scene in their towns too. The implications are far-reaching and difficult to calculate. How many people had their perceptions of how things are done changed by a laid-back, friendly Hope gig? How many people got involved with music because Hope gigs made it seem so much more accessible and affordable? How many friendships were forged? All the touring bands who might never have gotten a chance to visit Ireland otherwise? How many people became politicized, became vegetarian, even?

I feel Hope did all the hard work back when Dublin was grim and everything was about the next **U2**.

The way I saw the Hope Collective doing things has influenced the way I do things. There was a sense of honesty. People talk about wanting an alternative to corporate rock but in reality they crave the trappings, the guest list, special treatment, being idolized. There was none of that bullshit in Hope, and I try to continue in this manner.

I can definitely say that the existence of the Hope Collective and involvement with it has profoundly affected my lifestyle and outlook today. I hope their legacy continues for a long time to come."

—*Derek Byrne*

LIST OF GIGS

Officially Hope gigs from August 1989

1984—1988

June 1 '84	Vicarious Living, Support	Tommy Dunne's
July 13 '85	Trocaire Benefit	CIE Hall
April 7 '86	Membranes, Paranoid Visions, Kill Devil Hill	Belvedere Hotel
June 9 '87	P.U.L.P. (Hope)	JJ Smyths
June 16 '87	P.U.L.P. (Hope)	JJ Smyths
May 15 '88	Membranes, Pleasure Cell, Not Our World	Connolly Youth Hall
May 18 '88	Membranes, Not Our World	Underground
May 20 '88	Membranes, Not Our World, A House, Louis Stewart	Christchurch Cathedral
Nov. 29 '88	Fugazi, Three Ring Psychosis, Moral Crusade, N.O.W.	McGonagles

1989

Feb. 17	N.O.W., Banished, Angus, House Of Byron	Grattan
Feb. 24	N.O.W., Keltic Konviction, Malicious Damage, Lawnmowers	Grattan
March 10	Anhrefn, Not Our World	UCD
March 11	Anhrefn, Not Our World	Grattan
May 19	Anhrefn, Not Our World, Keltic Konviction	Man Of Arran
August 8	Vandals, 3 Ring Psychosis, Not Our World	Grattan
August 8	Vandals, Not Our World	Sides
Oct. 23	Antic Hay, Bloody Jellies, Flying Kidney	Grattan
Nov. 23	Fugazi, Slowest Clock, Not Our World	McGonagles

1990

March 13	D.I., The fFlaps (cancelled on night)	New Inn
April 24	Nomeansno, N.O.W., Killercrust, Trenchtown, Sloth	New Inn
June 7	Babydigger, Lawnmowers	New Inn
June 29	Jailcell Recipes, Drive, FUAL	New Inn
Sept. 15	Fugazi, The Rhythm-ites, Therapy?	McGonagles
Nov. 25	Firewater Creed, Lethargic, Renegade	Attic
Dec. 2	Therapy?, Shred, Pig Ignorance	Attic
Dec. 9	Whipping Boy, House Of Byron, The Grown Ups	Attic
Dec. 16	Sloth	Attic
Dec. 23	The Umbrellas	Attic
Dec. 30	Suburban Rebels, Violent Phobia	Attic

1991

Jan. 18	Cowboy Killers	NCAD
Jan. 19	Cowboy Killers, Shred, Paranoid Visions	Attic
Jan. 21	Cowboy Killers, Paranoid Visions	Grattan
Feb. 1	Splintered	UCD
Feb. 2	Splintered, Paranoid Visions, The Grown Ups	Charlie's
Feb. 24	Quicksand	Bolton St.

Feb. 24	Quicksand, Sloth	Charlie's
Feb. 25	Quicksand, Skin Horses, Afflicted	Grattan
March 9	Jailcell Recipes, Force Fed	Charlie's
March 16	Herb Garden, Village Idiots, Ciunas	Charlie's
March 30	AC Temple, Shred	Charlie's
April 13	Gorilla Biscuits, Drive, Unsound	Charlie's
April 16	The Keatons, Tension, I Am The Waltons	Charlie's
May 18	FUAL, Coitus, Paranoid Visions, Ciunas	Charlie's
May 23	Ogre, Shred, Stone Pony, Tension	Fox + Pheasant
May 30	Grown Ups, Onion Breath, Jam Jar Jail, Pet Lamb	Fox + Pheasant
June 1	NOFX, Go!, Decline	Charlie's
June 3	NOFX, Afflicted, Farside, Gumph	Fox + Pheasant
June 22	Inside Out, In Motion, Mexican Pets	Charlie's
July 13	Econochrist, World Of Drums, Jam Jar Jail	Charlie's
July 15	Econochrist, The Grown Ups, Ciunas	Fox + Pheasant
July 20	Babes In Toyland, Pet Lamb	Charlie's
July 22	Babes In Toyland, In Motion	Fox + Pheasant
August 5	Headcleaner, The Grown Ups, Pig Ignorance	Fox + Pheasant
Sept. 15	Nomeansno, Pet Lamb, Tension	McGonagles
Sept. 21	DFA, In Motion, The Crowd	Charlie's
Sept. 28	Aim, Sink, Stigmatamartyr	Charlie's
Sept. 30	Sink	Bolton
Oct. 5	Anhrefn, Negu Gorriak	Charlie's
Oct. 11	Sons Of Ishmael, Turtle Assasins, Arnheim	Fox + Pheasant
Oct. 19	Slum Turkeys, In Motion	Charlie's
Oct. 22	Slum Turkeys	Trinity College
Oct. 24	Slum Turkeys, Mexican Pets	Barnstormers
Oct. 31	Jam Jar Jail, Pitch Shifter, Dust Revolution	Fox + Pheasant
Oct. 31	Pitchshifter, Golden Horde	NCAD
Nov. 5	The Ex, Dog Faced Hermans	Fox + Pheasant
Nov. 5	The Ex	Waterfront
Dec. 15	Green Day, Dog Day	Attic

1992

Jan. 20	Slunk, Tension	Barnstormers
Jan. 21	Slunk	Bolton St.
Jan. 24	Slunk, Onion Breath, Arnheim	Fox + Pheasant
Feb. 23	Decadence Within, Alumni Feedback, World Of Drums	Attic
March 8	Nessun Dorma, Zygote	Grattan
March 19	Spermbirds, Onion Breath, SMH	Barnstormers
March 21	Spiny Norman Quartet	Barnstormers
April 4	Decline, Jailcell Recipes, Unsound	Barnstormers
April 23	Wat Tyler, Thatcher On Acid	Fibber Magees
April 26	Wat Tyler, Thatcher On Acid, Dog Day	Barnstormers
May 11	Chumbawamba	Trinity College
May 11	Fugazi, Chumbawamba, In Motion	SFX
May 31	NOFX, Gas Farm, Arnheim	Barnstormers

June 26	Instigators, Brinskill Bombbeat, Bike Thieves	The Roxey
July 4	Mr. T. Experience, Dog Day	Barnstormers
July 19	Headcleaner, Crossbreed	Barnstormers
August 1	MDC, Ciunas	Barnstormers
August 15	Heavenly, Pecadilloes	Barnstormers
August 23	Decadence Within, Herb Garden, The Collectors	Barnstormers
August 30	Alice Donut, Gout, Brawl	Barnstormers
Sept. 11	Dawson, Long Fin Killie	Barnstormers
Sept. 17	Crane, Mexican Pets	Fibber Magees
Sept. 18	Crane	Our Price
Sept. 20	Crane, Mexican Pets	Barnstormers
Sept. 26	Jawbreaker, Collectors, Ace,	Barnstormers
Oct. 9	Revenge Of The Carrots, Donkey	Barnstormers
Oct. 29	Dog Day, Groundswell	Fleet
Nov. 4	Downcast, Groundswell	Barnstormers
Nov. 5	Pecadilloes, Wormhole	Fleet
Nov. 8	Surf Weasel, Blue Babies	Mulligans
Nov. 12	Surf Weasel, Unease	Fleet
Dec. 13	Shanks, Treehouse	Fleet

1993

Jan. 14	Luggage, Wormhole	Fleet
Jan. 21	Manson's Garden, Grin	Fleet
Jan. 28	Lice Woman, Golden Mile	Fleet
Feb. 24	Headcleaner, Holemasters	Barnstormers
Feb. 28	Cornershop, Wheel, Jam Jar Jail	Fibber Magees
March 6	Life But How To Live It, Dirt, Onion Breath, Female Hercules	Mulligans
May 10	Down By Law, Wheel, Groundswell	Barnstormers
May 24	Headcleaner, Slunk, Flexihead	Barnstormers
August 18	Dawson, Long Fin Killie, Pet Lamb	Attic
August 25	Brawl	Attic
Sept. 6	Holy Rollers	Barnstormers
Oct. 8	Golden Mile, Flexihead, In Motion, Groundswell	Barnstormers
Nov. 5	Neurosis, Ciunas	Barnstormers
Nov. 11	Frank Sidebottom	Barnstormers
Nov. 21	Oi Polloi	Barnstormers
Dec. 1	Herb Garden	Barnstormers
Dec. 2	Herb Garden	UCD
Dec. 23	Gan, The Revs, Wheel	Attic

1994

Feb. 22	Circus Lupus, Lungfish, Flexihead	Barnstormers
April 29	Grotus, Victims Family	Barnstormers
June 10	Pitchshifter, Dub War	Fox + Pheasant
June 7	Nomeanso, Manhole, Mexican Pets	Furnace
Oct. 25	Jawbreaker, Sinch	Furnace

1996

March 29	Cheapskate, Gout, Brian Bannon, Stomach	Attic
April 6	Underfoot, Nurse Diesel, Jackbeast	Attic
April 20	Bikini Kill, Team Dresch, Bis	Charlie's
May 28	Gameface, Cleanslate, Pincher Martin,	
	Blood Or Whiskey	DA Club
June 15	Carnivore 7, Cheapskate, Brooder	Attic
June 29	Lithium Joe, Cranc, Norvics	Attic
August 10	Bull Taco, Frankie Stubbs	City Arts Centre
August 14	Des Man DeAblo	Attic
August 15	Relapse, Capratone, The Slippies, Pet Lamb	City Arts Centre
August 17	Consume, Monkhouse, Brooder, Blunt	City Arts Centre
Sept. 6	Polaris, Loretta, Jackbeast	Attic
Sept. 13	Down By Law	Attic
Sept. 29	Citizen Fish, Cheapskate, Dysfunctional	Charlie's
Oct. 16	Los Crudos, Ebola, Holo-Christ, Relapse	Attic
Nov. 5	Drop Dead, Neckweed, Jackbeast	Attic
Dec 7	Stomach, Bambi, Cheapskate, Blackbelt Jones	Attic
Dec. 13	Jackbeast, The Steam Pig, Porn, Brian Bannon, Yawn	Attic

1997

Feb. 10	The VSS, Brooder, Holemasters	Fusion
Feb. 23	Vide Physique, Headache, Jobbykrust	Fusion
March 26	Kito, Bilgepump, Jackbeast	Underground
April 24	Gout, Stomach, Black Belt Jones	Charlie's
May 2	State of Fear, Cheapskate, Puget Sound	Charlie's
May 9	Waltons, Striknien DC, Steam Pig, Brinskill Bomb Beat	Charlie's
June 22	Sparkmarker, The Kabinboy, Blackbelt Jones	Charlie's
June 29	Month of Birthdays, Capstan, Tetsuo	Charlie's
July 15	Bloco Vomit, Roaring Silence, Noise Pollution	Fusion
August 16	Wat Tyler, Fat Day, Black Belt Jones, Cheapskate	City Arts Centre
August 17	Jesse, Jackbeast, The Waltons, Hylton Weir, The Null Set	City Arts Centre
August 24	Abhinanda, Starmarket, Neckweed	Fusion
Sep. 21	Hal Al Shedad, Castles & Car Wrecks, Bambi	Fusion
Oct. 26	Bluetip, Kerosene 454, Jackbeast, Hylton Weir	Fusion
Nov. 8	The Van Pelt, The Sin Eaters, Blackbelt Jones, O	Fusion
Dec. 6	The Sorts, The Redneck Manifesto	Funnel

1998

January 23	Cheapskate, Stomach, Debt	Fusion
Feb. 13	The Kabinboy, Residence, Blackbelt Jones	Fusion
Feb. 27	Masamba, Joan of Arse, Franci	Fusion
March 13	One Car Pile Up, Vanilla Pod, Dissent	Fusion
April 25	Consume, Conscious, Residence	Fusion
May 23	Refused, Ink & Dagger, Hylton Weir	McGraths
June 28	Duffy Moon, Machine Gun Etiquette, The Juniors	Fusion
Sept. 4	Abhinanda, Residence, Low End	Fusion

Oct. 27	Polaris, Null Set, Hylton Weir	Funnel
Nov. 26	Drop Dead, John Holmes	Clodaghs Flat
Dec. 6	The Sorts, The Redneck Manifesto	Funnel

1999

March 26	Bluetip, The Farewell Bend, The Redneck Manifesto	Funnel
April 17	Month of Birthdays, Capstan, Joan of Arse, Estel	Funnel
May 28	Happy Anger, The Null Set, Sir Killalot	Fusion
July 13	Astream, Dropnose, Sir Killalot	Slatterys
Nov. 6	Milgram, The Rednecck Manifesto, Estel	Isaac Butts
Nov. 13	Bluetip (with Bambi at their 7" launch)	Isaac Butts
Dec. 7	The Sorts, Joan of Arse	JJ Smyths

John Holmes

DOCUMENT: A POSTSCRIPT

The idea for this book first arose in 1996, six years before publication, at a Hope Collective meeting. It was agreed that what happened during a certain time in Dublin should be documented. I agreed to take on the task.

During the initial process, as detailed in the book, the Hope Collective fizzled out. When my daughter Ellen was a year old I decided to relight the fire. I spent endless months on the Internet pretending I was a private detective. I tried to contact all the 283 bands that played a Hope gig. Some were to prove elusive. Old acquaintances were renewed and I became a pest to certain band members. The same few lines—"Hi . . . Remember me, I was involved in putting your band on in Dublin. I'm doing a book about it. Can you send me a vegan recipe or an anecdote about your time here? Oh yeah, hope all has been well in your life for the past 10 years ..."—were rolled out.

Most people were interested and said they'd get back to me, some ignored me and some cast me aside as a freak. My family was starting to forget what I looked like and phone bills quadrupled. I set a deadline to try and rush people into fulfilling their promise to submit something. This and many other deadlines were set and missed. Our second child was born and my priorities were rearranged once more.

However, this book wouldn't have been possible without Lee Casey coming in to help. Lee offered to write an introduction for the book. He was then enlisted to help trace down some people. That assistance has grown and he has been invaluable in getting this book past the final hurdle. The first time I met Lee was in McGonagles in 1988. He gave me a tape of his band and asked could they play a gig sometime. They played soon after and we have been friends since. This is a common occurrence through gigs, no matter who is putting them on.

Will and Ricky from Belfast Gig Collective offered to do the cover. They are Ricky's photos and Will designs his own magazine so to get them involved was an honour.

Other photos in the book belong to George Curran. His photos are from earlier gigs and are integral to the book.

Many people made *Please Feed Me* possible.

Everyone who went to Hope gigs, supported what we were trying to do and did something constructive to help. Through all this there has been the never-ending love and assistance from my family. For my parents, when I was at home sick, they always supported what I wanted to do. For my brothers, who acted as security, chauffeurs and secretaries. For Hugo, who brought The Membranes over first. For Paddy, Alan, Fergus, Richie who helped out with Fugazi the first time. For Valerie, the Bearded Lady and Miriam who were the main backers from 1989–1994. For Pete, Finbar, Derek, Anthony, Clodagh, Eugene, Jamie and the entire Hope Collective who carried the torch for a while. For those endless patient people in places like Monaghan, Arklow, Cork, Dundalk, Antrim, Kilkenny, Kill, New Ross, Limerick, Galway, Letterkenny, Larne, Belfast, Derry and Waterford who created their own Hope. Thank you. It was wonderful.

Thanks to all the people who contributed. It really is appreciated. A last word goes out to my best friend and wife for her endless patience, help and support. Thank you, Mir.

—Niall McGuirk, July 2002

APPENDIX: WEIGHTS, MEASURES & TERMS

Because European recipes often use weight instead of volume to measure ingredients and because these ingredients sometimes go by names unfamiliar to those over here, a number of the recipes in this book have been Americanized in order to keep the math away from the knives. Below are some of the more common conversions just in case you need to switch back sometime.

WEIGHT & VOLUME

I pound (16 oz) = 450 g
I cup water = 1/4 litre (8 fl. oz)
I tbsp. butter = 1/2 oz
I cup wheat, self rising flour = 126g (4 3/8 oz)
I cup chick pea flour = 92 g (3 1/4 oz)
I cup creamed coconut = 3 oz.
I cup sugar = 7 1/8 oz
I cup margarine = 8 3/8 oz
I cup chopped walnuts = 4 1/8 oz
I cup vegetable stock = 1/2 pint
I cup lentils = 125 g
I cup oatmeal = 87.5 g
I cup dried pears = 125 g
I cup vegetables = 100 g (approx.)

HEAT

225 F = 110 C = Gas Mark 1/4
250 F = 130 C = Gas Mark 1/2
275 F = 140 C = Gas Mark 1
300 F = 150 C = Gas Mark 2
325 F = 170 C = Gas Mark 3
350 F = 180 C = Gas Mark 4
375 F = 190 C = Gas Mark 5
400 F = 200 C = Gas Mark 6
425 F = 220 C = Gas Mark 7
450 F = 230 C = Gas Mark 8
475 F = 240 C = Gas Mark 9

$C = \frac{5}{9}(F\text{-}32)$

TERMS

whole wheat bread = whole meal bread
eggplant = aubergine
zucchini = courgette
penne pasta = pasta quills
baking soda = bicarbonate of soda
fresh cilantro = coriander leaves
bell peppers = peppers
molasses = treacle
pitted olives = destoned olives
tortillas = burrito wrappers
golden raisins = sultanas
lima beans = butter beans
rutabega = swede
corn starch = corn flour
soy hamburger = soya minee
romaine lettuce = kos lettuce
pizza crust = pizza base

It's strange for me writing this and having to explain two food institutions for you. It shows that although the world may seem like a small place at times we really are a world apart at others. Look in the food press (you may call them cupboards) in any house in Ireland and you will find brown sauce. If there are people under 40 in the house there will be a pot noodle.

Brown sauce is the black sheep of the tomato ketchup family. Spicy and no tomatoes but with the same consistency, I've heard you may call it steak sauce but we use it with our potatoes in Ireland.

Pot Noodles is a dehydrated mixture of pasta and vegetables that sparkle to life with the addition of hot water. It comes in a plastic dish, you just add the water, add the flavour sachet and leave it for a couple of minutes. It may not be nutritious but it sure is delicious.

—Niall

Printed in the United States
by Baker & Taylor Publisher Services